Irish Management Briefings

DEALING WITH CHANGE

THE LESSONS FOR IRISH MANAGERS

Tom McConalogue

www.oaktreepress.com

Oak Tree Press
19 Rutland Street
Cork, Ireland
http://www.oaktreepress.com

© 2003 Tom McConalogue

A catalogue record of this book is
available from the British Library.

ISBN 1-86076-273-5

All rights reserved. No part of this publication may be reproduced or
transmitted in any form or by any means, including photocopying and
recording, without written permission of the publisher. Such written permission
must also be obtained before any part of this publication is stored in a retrieval
system of any nature. Requests for permission should be directed to
Oak Tree Press, 19 Rutland Street, Cork, Ireland.

Edited and typeset by Emer Ryan/David Houlden
Printed by eprint, Dublin, Ireland
e-mail: books@e-print.ie

16036

CONTENTS

ACKNOWLEDGEMENTS

The author would like to acknowledge a debt of gratitude to those who provided access to their organisations as case examples, and to those managers who made time to share their reflections on what for many was an intense and personal experience. Also, many thanks to those who completed the questionnaires that allowed the report to reflect a broader view of what is currently happening in Irish organisations.

While it is hoped that the organisations and managers featured in this briefing are not misrepresented, the author takes full responsibility for the interpretation of the data and the conclusions reported.

INTRODUCTION

The well-known aphorism, "nothing is so certain as change", has become an increasing reality for Irish organisations in the past decade. While a recent survey by Carlson Marketing and Gallup[1] reports seven out of ten US managers identifying their organisations as having gone through a major reorganisation in the past five years, more than 80 per cent of Irish managers report similar levels of change within the past two years, and many anticipate even shorter time frames in the future. Thanks in good measure to the Celtic Tiger, most organisations in Ireland must not only learn to manage the increasing complexity of their operational demands, but also sustain a cycle of continuous improvement interspersed with periodic discontinuous change.

However, while change has become almost a byword, there is very little information on how Irish organisations and managers anticipate and implement their change efforts. Many of the reported accounts of change are selective and anecdotal, tending to emphasise the tangible components such as restructuring or new technology, to the neglect of the human dimension. They also frequently identify transition with heroic leaders, while discounting the contribution of other staff in the process. Moreover, although many of the popular accounts of organisational change have been upbeat and self-promoting, there is increasing data to suggest that many transition efforts are less than successful in achieving the results they set out to deliver.

A Harvard study which tracked the change efforts of the Fortune 100 companies found that although most of them had implemented costly change programmes in the previous fifteen years, only 30 per cent had produced any significant improvement in bottom-line results.[2] A survey, by Atticus, of more than 400 leading international organisations, reported similar success rates of around 30 per cent, suggesting that failure to deliver on change is a global phenomenon.[3] Other research confirms a growing scepticism about the implementation of programmed approaches to change. Evidence on programmed approaches to change includes a study by the American Quality Association and Ernst and Young which found that most TQM programmes had not worked, while Hammer and Champy, the gurus of Business Process Re-engineering, were forced to admit that over 70 per cent of BPR projects were unsuccessful.[4] Furthermore, while information technology has been one of the main drivers of change in the Irish economy over the past ten years, research by Clegg and others indicates that more than 40 per cent of IT projects are abandoned and 90 per cent fail to deliver the benefits they promise.[5]

The growing body of knowledge on change management and the lack of success of many change projects begs two questions: "Why are many change efforts apparently less than effective?" and, considering the turbulent environment and rapid growth of the Irish economy, "To what extent are our organisations learning to deal with change?"

This Management Briefing sets out to inform and, it is hoped, to educate Irish managers on the critical success factors in anticipating and managing change. The three main questions it seeks to answer are:

1.   What kind of changes are Irish organisations experiencing and how are they responding?

2.   What has helped and what has blocked Irish organisations from managing change in the past?

3.   What are some of the essential lessons for Irish companies in anticipating and managing change for the future?

Much of the information in this report was gained from a series of in-depth interviews with thirty managers in five organisations that have undergone major change in the past five years. They included Waterford Crystal, ESB Powergen, The Equality Investigations Agency, The ITG Group and Irish Life. In addition, a questionnaire (see Appendix) was also used to gather data from 130 managers, representing a broad range of public and private organisations. Finally, data was also collected from seven organisation-development consultants, in the expectation that they would provide a more measured view of how well Irish organisations are learning to manage change.

Chapter 1 gives a brief outline of the Irish economy and how its development has influenced the management of change. Chapter 2 identifies the main external drivers for change and the variety of organisational responses to those influences, while Chapter 3 looks at the main approaches and techniques organisations use in responding to change. Chapter 4 identifies the main blocks to change and how those blocks can be better managed, while Chapter 5 reports conclusions on how organisations could better manage change, and outlines the lessons that still need to be learned. Finally, Chapter 6 looks to the future of organisational change and change management, and suggests areas where Irish organisations need to focus their efforts.

The briefing is interspersed with case examples from Irish companies that are at different stages of growth — some in the early stages of their development, recognising that the need for change comes early in the life of many organisations. Several of the cases illustrate the challenges that have been pursued by Irish organisations in creating and sustaining a culture of agility and learning, while others illustrate how mature organisations are struggling to create readiness for change and transformation.

1

THE EXTERNAL ENVIRONMENT

Whether in manufacturing or in services, the public or the private sector, most Irish organisations have experienced a considerable amount of change in the past decade. With a likelihood of continued economic growth in Ireland and turbulence in the global economy in the form of new technology, environmental legislation, price fluctuations and political upheavals, successful organisations will be those that develop sustainable strategies for managing change and an ability to make quick responses to fluctuations in the environment.

1.1 THE GLOBAL ECONOMY

While there have been many external influences on the Irish economy over the past decade, the main effects of the environment have been threefold. Firstly, although Ireland has moved in the past three decades from a closed economy, heavily dependent on agriculture, to a mixed economy that includes agri-business, financial services, manufacturing and tourism, along the way it has become increasingly dependent on foreign investment. While the 1,100 foreign companies currently operating in Ireland create direct employment in excess of 116,000 jobs, they indirectly seed a similar volume of employment through spin-off activities in the form of outsourcing, subcontracting and the multiplier effect. With a current workforce of 1.8 million, Ireland is dependent on foreign investment for up to 20 per cent of its jobs and, as a consequence, is more vulnerable than most countries to the vagaries of the multinationals, the fortunes of the US and EU economies and the liberalisation of trade and commerce in the rest of the world

Secondly, the Irish economy is essentially export driven. Since the early days of industrialisation, like other developing countries with a small domestic market — Korea, for example — the mainstay of growth in Ireland has been exports, which reached £65.4 billion in 2001, almost trebling since 1995. With a sustained annual increase of more than 15 per cent in the value of exports over the past decade (a 72 per cent rise in volume), the main growth areas for exports have been in chemicals and high technology, including the manufacture of computers, components and software. Other significant areas of growth have been in service provision, particularly in the finance and information sectors which now account for a quarter of all exports. However, while Ireland has achieved a commendable record of export growth, we have also become more vulnerable to cost competition (computer manufacture), consumer power (meat embargoes), and political influence (the relocation of Digital).

FIGURE 1.1 — IMPORTS AND EXPORTS

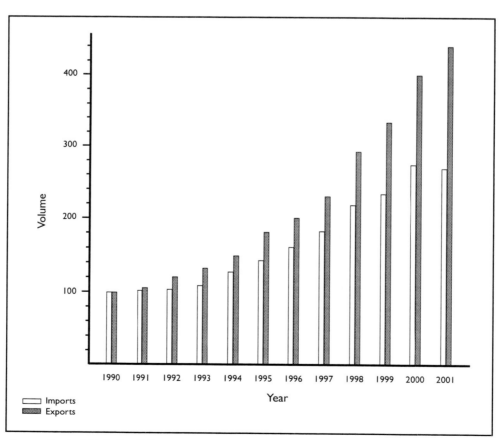

Source: Central Statistics Office

More fundamental, however, than our openness to inward investment and the increasing volume of exports has been the growth in information technology and communications. Not only has information and communications technology (ICT) reduced our geographic isolation, it has also allowed Ireland to leapfrog many of the more mature economies in the transition to newer high-tech and knowledge-based industries. Ireland has also created its own advantages for growth by encouraging inward investment and export growth through tax incentives and investment grants, and by setting up greenfield institutions to support that development. In education, for example, while colleges like Dublin City University and the University of Limerick have geared themselves to produce a steady stream of technical and business graduates for the knowledge and service sectors, a broad explosion in third-level education has contributed to building a confidence in Irish businesses that they have access to the resources necessary to compete successfully in the global marketplace.

The degree of organisational learning that has accompanied the more open and global environment is also significant. Not only has the influx of foreign-owned companies brought new styles of managing, explicit ethics and values, participative work practices and a customer-driven ethos, but it has also stimulated a learning process in many of the home-grown companies. State-of-the-art HRM practices, sophisticated management-development systems and opportunities for international experience have all served to create a mind-set designed to attract and retain good staff, where innovation is seen as a constant and where managers do not have to be convinced that change should not be imposed or settled through negotiation.

1.2 THE IRISH ECONOMY

In a few short years, the Irish economy has gone through a major transformation which is reflected in the many transitions experienced by individual organisations. In the late 1970s, Ireland had cast itself in the role of the "Celtic Pauper", with debts in excess of 120 per cent of GNP, the financial statistics of a third-world country and a begging bowl mentality. The economy was under performing, the population was overtaxed; there were high levels of unemployment and there was a real threat of returning to the mass emigration of the 1950s. The Irish economy did not need to create a crisis to stimulate change — it already had one.

While no single initiative can be singled out as having triggered the growth rates of the past decade — in excess of double the EU average — several important factors have contributed to the phenomenon of the "Celtic Tiger". A growing realisation that the *mé féin* mentality of protectionism, trade barriers and exchange controls had served the country badly in the past encouraged people to embrace the European ideal in 1973 with an 83 per cent "yes" vote for EEC membership. Our active participation and positive attitude towards the EU (with the exception of Nice) has had a major impact on seeding many of the economic and social changes needed to move from an inward-looking society to a more open economy. Similarly, the development of sound economic and fiscal policies and the creation of an infrastructure for growth, including agencies like the IDA and FÁS, a more open third-level education system and partnership agreements with the trades unions have also contributed to making Ireland a thriving export economy and attractive for overseas investment — with 1 per cent of the population of the EU, Ireland currently attracts over 20 per cent of all inward investment.

1.3 FUTURE GROWTH

With a recent downturn in the US economy and the catastrophic events of 11 September 2001 and the global war on terrorism, the long-term effects on the Irish economy are difficult to predict. Industrial production was already falling before 11 September, notably in the information technology sector, with lay-offs and the closure of companies like Gateway and General Semiconductors. Other areas of the economy have also been affected by recent events, reflected in a sharp decline in the airline business and tourism — the North American market typically accounting for a million visitors each year and a potential spend of almost €700 million.

However, although there has been a great deal of speculation about the prospects for economic growth in the next decade, both the ESRI and OECD continue to predict a positive future for the Irish economy, with a couple of years of slow growth followed by an increase towards the end of 2003. Recent reports also suggest that the recession in the US is less deep than predicted and, in the past months, it has been showing some signs of recovery. Nevertheless, while many of the current performance indicators favour a climate of continued growth, there are signs to suggest that the growth cycle of the past decade is unlikely to continue. The proposed enlargement of the EU, the emergence of Eastern Europe with its low-cost workforce, current levels of inflation at home and the appreciation of the Euro against the US dollar and the UK pound are some of the weak signals which suggest that growth will have to be more internally driven for the future. No longer are the demands of Maastricht or investment grants and tax-free breaks sufficient to fuel the economy — future growth can be sustained only through individual organisations and institutions learning how to manage their transitions in anticipation of continued turbulence and periodic dramatic shifts in the environment.

FIGURE 1.2 — UNEMPLOYMENT RATES 1988–2002

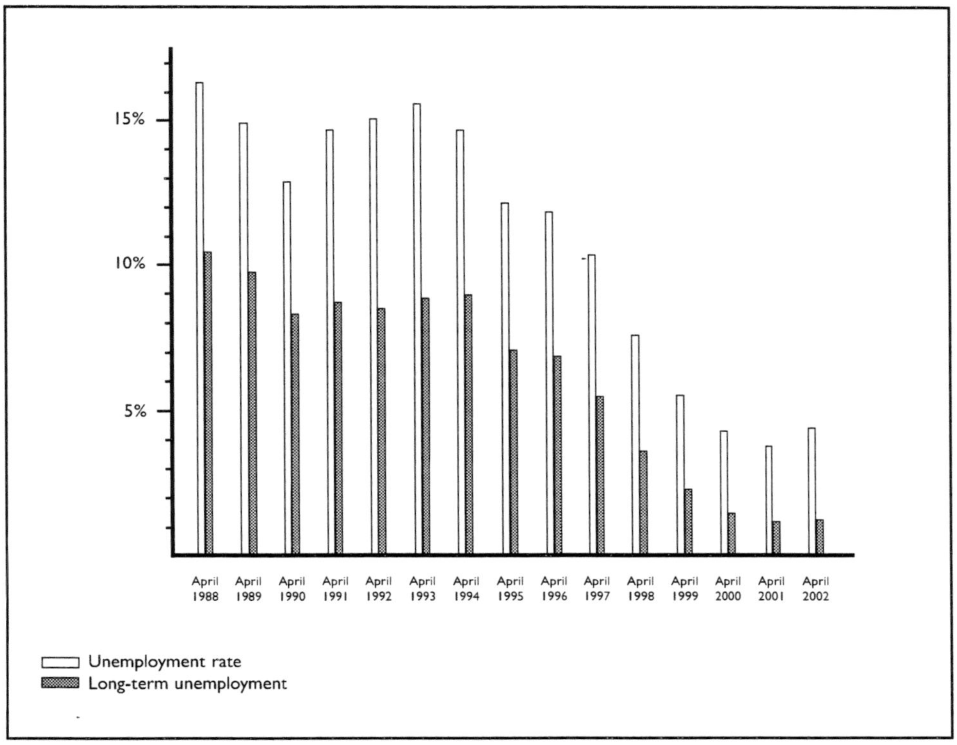

Source: Central Statistics Office

1.4 HISTORICAL RESPONSES TO CHANGE

During the 1950s and 1960s, as Ireland emerged from its post-war isolation, organisational changes tended to reflect a static environment and were aimed at creating jobs and improving efficiencies through cost reduction and economies of scale. Growth was slow and there was little industrial unrest — people were grateful to have a job and those who had no job emigrated.

Several studies used the McKinsey 7's framework as a basis for comparing organisations in the same industry. They indicated that the main distinguishing features of successful companies lay in the softer areas of shared vision, service, style and human resource practices. The 7's model also suggests the need for alignment between the hard and soft areas, suggesting that misalignments can have a profound effect on an organisation's ability to manage its own changes. For example, many companies that tried to introduce TQM or BPR failed because they lacked a shared value around quality or a culture of improvement.

Hard s's	**Soft s's**
Strategy	Staff
Systems	Shared values
Structure	Skills
Style	

In the following decade, as foreign-owned companies and multi-nationals (MNCs) began to establish themselves, the global environment saw a virtual assault on western markets by Japanese companies. Many of the popular writings of the time, such as *The Art of Japanese Management*[1] and *In Search of Excellence*[2] reflected a growing disillusionment with western models of organisation and change. The emerging view was that the main competitive advantage for the future would lie in the softer areas, captured by Jack Welch of GE in the phrase "soft values for a hard decade". Staff and customers who were historically seen as the least important ingredient in organisational success started to be seen as the most critical.

A growing body of evidence began to suggest that culture, values and attitudes were just as important to success as technology or strategy. As a result, we have seen in the past twenty years a much greater emphasis on changing the softer areas of organisation, such as quality, customer service and innovation. Combined with the increasing shortage of knowledge workers, this new emphasis has encouraged many organisations to focus on realising the full potential of their staff through training and encouraging new attitudes, increased participation and empowerment. Furthermore, as a reflection of that shift, while the predominant change models prior to the 1980s came from the physical sciences, in recent years there has been more attraction to behavioural science models and frameworks that place a much greater emphasis on the human aspects of change and on the psychological aspects of transition.

FIGURE 1.3 — MIGRATION

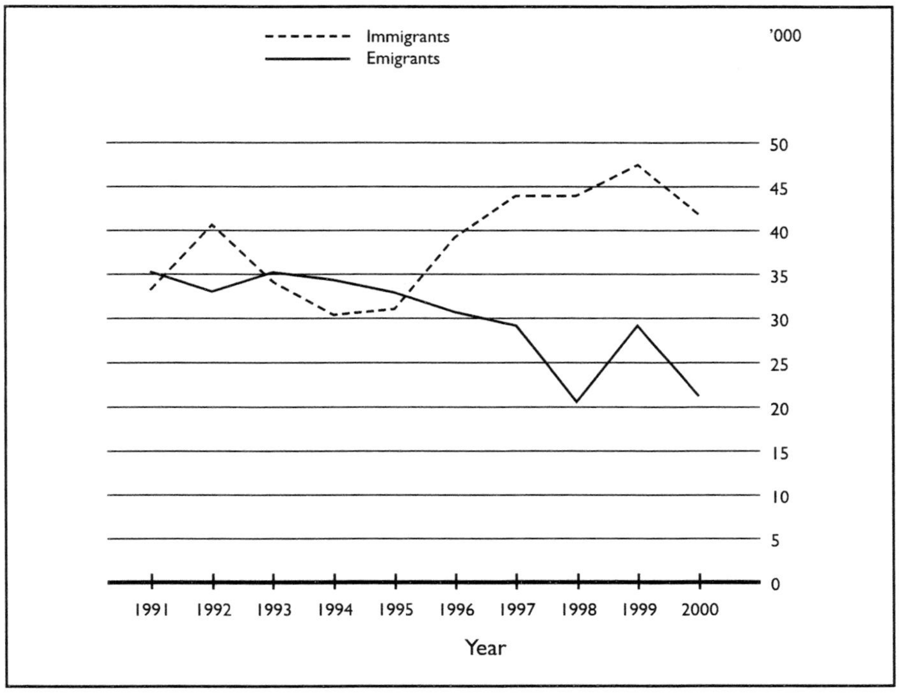

Source: Central Statistics Office

In discussing the changing approaches to change in Irish businesses, it is interesting to examine how they reflect the various stages of our economic and social development. In the fledgling economy of the late 1960s and early 1970s, most change in the private sector was by decree or, at least, top down. In the public and semi-state sector, change was mainly the product of consultants' reports, which invariably recommended restructuring, changes in work practices and reductions in staffing. The focus of such change efforts reflected the prevailing culture of productivity bargaining, which included expert diagnosis, negotiation and compensation for change. It added to the growing division and mistrust between staff and management, reflected in a number of deep and damaging strikes during that period — banks, postal services and electricity, for example.

In the late 1970s, with the arrival of the first MNCs such as Pfizer and Digital, the emergence of human resource professionals, and the popularising of Japanese management practices, many change efforts were directed at gaining the benefits of the new manufacturing and people management systems such as *kaizen*, JIT, TQM and Quality Circles. In the early to mid-1980s, a proliferation of writings on turnaround management and transformational leadership also reflected a reality that, in the wake of global competition and deregulation, many organisations that had previously been protected from competition were going into almost terminal decline before being rescued in dramatic ways by new leadership and radical restructuring. Although it took some time for organisations to look beyond the quick fix of decline and turnaround, an emerging emphasis on the customer and quality began to wean the management mind-set away from a preoccupation with internal efficiencies and control to a more external focus on the customer and the competition.

	1950s & 1960s	1970s & 1980s	1990s & 2000
Environment	Stable ∀	Uncertain ∀	Turbulent ∀
Planning	Incremental ∀	Short term ∀	Contingency ∀
Focus	Efficiency ∀	Results ∀	Customer ∀
Style	Administration ∀	Management ∀	Leadership ∀

During this period, as newly industrialised countries like Korea and Taiwan began to demonstrate that most products, from computers to cars, were commodities that could be manufactured at very competitive prices in low-wage economies, it became increasingly clear that future competitive advantage for Ireland lay in the knowledge and service areas. However, while some Irish organisations took to heart the lessons of product quality and customer service, many were left wondering how to create a culture of excellence if not through half-hearted slogans, creative mission statements, expensive programmes for change, and using consultants to teach staff the softer skills of customer service, quality and teamwork.

Only in the late 1980s and early 1990s did many Irish companies begin to recognise that programmed approaches to change were often expensive and ineffective and that restructurings or turnaround were strategies that organisations could use only occasionally. It led many to the conclusion that getting real and sustainable change required the commitment and involvement of those who were likely to be affected. Reflecting a view that healthy change is consensual and that most change efforts are ultimately about changing values, norms, attitudes and behaviours, as well as systems or technology, many Irish organisations have begun to accept the need for managers and staff to take ownership for change by actively involving them in the planning and implementation processes.

Since the mid-1990s, a growing acceptance that turbulence and uncertainty will be ongoing features of the economy for the future has also led many companies to recognise the need to develop permanent cultures of continuous improvement (CIP) and change (Learning Organisations). Important writings like *The Fifth Discipline*[3] and *The Living Company*,[4] and the lessons from organisations that have developed a resilience to change — such as IBM, Marriot and Intel — have helped to generate an interest in designing organisational architecture that preserves the core mission and values, while allowing for flexibility and resilience to the changing environment.

However, while there are encouraging signs that many Irish organisations are developing new skills and competencies for managing change, others are still trapped in a mind-set which sees change in terms of restructuring and reducing numbers of staff, negotiated agreements based on incentives and compensation, programmed approaches such as ISO and TQM, and "sheep-dip" solutions such as putting all the staff through service or quality programmes. In response to signs of major changes in the global environment, such as new communications technology and the ease of doing business across national frontiers, the way that Irish organisations manage change for the future will also have to mature and change.

1.5 CURRENT AND FUTURE RESPONSES

In line with a view that "the future is now", many of the characteristics required by Irish organisations for the future are clearly evident in the way that they now operate. While the introduction of new technologies, flexible structures and sophisticated systems has enabled a great deal of change to take place, some of the main effects have been on the culture of Irish organisations. Not only have many organisations learned that their competitive advantages increasingly lies in the speed and quality of their response to customer needs and the competition, but they have also recognised that meeting those demands means empowering staff, modifying management styles, and encouraging real participation. Moreover, although the virtual organisation may be somewhere in the future, the changing circumstances have also led many businesses to refocus on their core activities while outsourcing many of the ancillary services, introducing flexible work arrangements, and offering a broad variety of opportunities to attract skilled staff and hold on to their best people.

While the trends in change management over the past four decades are well reflected in new thinking and creative approaches adopted by many Irish businesses, there is still a broad spread in where organisations are on the learning cycle. As reported in an earlier Oak Tree briefing, *Employee Partnership in Ireland*,[5] research by the Graduate School of Business in UCD concludes that while the dominant approach to change in unionised companies is collective bargaining on working conditions and pay, it has become increasingly popular for managers to deal directly with employees on changes in work practices. The broad indications are that while some organisations are still wedded to top-down approaches to change, others are using mixed models that include external bargaining and internally driven culture change processes, while yet others have moved to more participative and inclusive approaches where the stakeholders are involved and share in the benefits of change.

The next chapter will examine what drives Irish organisations to embark on change or decide to develop architecture to support a culture of sustainable change, and what strategies they use to bring about the changes they need and want to make.

2

THE DRIVERS AND RESPONSES TO CHANGE

2.1 EXTERNAL DRIVING FORCES

As living organisms learn to adapt to their changing environments rather than run the risk of extinction, so organisations have to learn that realignment and transition are healthy responses to changing political, economic and social circumstances. When conditions in the environment are relatively stable, those changes tend to happen in an evolutionary way, but in conditions of turbulence and rapid change, as seen in Ireland over the past decade, there is a need for much more radical responses.

Faced with a rapidly changing environment, organisations typically have three choices. They can soldier on with incremental change in the hope that the environment will return to a more settled state or they can go into slow decline, sometimes to the point where the only option is a turnaround strategy involving divesting parts of the business and radically reducing numbers of staff. Alternatively, a third choice for organisations is to develop the skills for managing periodic radical as well as ongoing incremental adjustments to keep the business aligned with its changing environment. While such options have traditionally applied to more mature business, many Irish organisations must now face those challenges much earlier in their life cycle and more dramatically than in previous decades.

MAIN EXTERNAL DRIVERS FOR CHANGE (RANK ORDER)

1. Increased levels and new competition
2. Technology and IT change and improvement
3. Increased demand for products and services
4. A new leader with a vision
5. Takeover/merger
6. High cost base
7. Customer dissatisfaction
8. Organisation or industry decline
9. Shareholder dissatisfaction

In essence, organisations change in order to survive and grow, and healthy organisations are those that anticipate and respond to changes in the environment rather than wait for a crisis to stimulate them into action. However, although many Irish organisations have been through a steep learning curve in the past decade, complacency still remains one of the main reasons for organisations drifting into decline, as seen in recent years with mature organisations like Aer Lingus and Iarnród Éireann. It is easy to speculate that many other Irish organisations would be similarly exposed by a downturn in the global economy and some have used the US recession and more recent events to do what they should probably have done much earlier.

> You really can miss the big picture out there — you can be easily seduced into believing that that all you have to do is tweak things — sometimes you have to come to terms with scrapping the existing system and starting again.

The main external drivers for change, as identified in the survey of 130 managers, include:

- Increased competition
- New technology and predictably
- Consumer demand for new products and services.

Increasing global competition has contributed in varying degrees to Irish companies becoming more focused, introducing better integrated and consumer friendly systems, casting more widely for trained staff, and investing heavily in training and management development. Growth in new technology — particularly in the IT area, with the computerisation of standard processes, the development of integrated systems such as SAP, and the increasing use of electronic transactions — has also been a major external driver for change. Not only has information technology greatly improved the ability of organisations to analyse and retrieve information; it has also provided many businesses with a major competitive advantage through better management of the supply chain, a reduction in marketing and distribution costs and by offering customers easier access to their products and services.

> The most significant change is globalisation of the market. This has traditionally been a high-cost industry — now there is competition from low-cost providers. It signals a new environment where the costs are going to be driven down.

However, while competition, new technologies and the growth of consumerism have been major driving forces for change, the Irish economy is still very dependent on exports for continuing growth, suggesting that global political and economic events are likely to have the greatest impact on Irish businesses in the future (the US was recently reported as having overtaken the UK as Ireland's largest export market). Moreover, while globalisation will continue as a major economic driver for the future, growth in consumer spending power has also seen the emergence of a more demanding home market, a better-educated workforce and a shift from labour-intensive manufacturing towards high-value-added goods and services. Also worthy of comment from the survey is that legislation, takeovers and mergers feature as significant drivers for change, suggesting that any external force which destabilises an organisation acts as a catalyst for change.

2.2 INTERNAL RESPONSES TO CHANGE

Before reporting on the responses that organisations make to their changing environments, it is worth defining three key characteristics of change: the organisational life cycle, the degree of change, and a process versus product view of change.

THE ORGANISATIONAL LIFE CYCLE

Organisations, like people, experience natural changes in their journey from youth to maturity. The start-up phase for most organisations is organic, with few policies and a simple structure, and, because of their size, a natural ability to adapt to the environment. During their growth and development stages, businesses tend to take on some of the more formal characteristics of organisation, such as specialist staff, more clearly defined and differentiated roles, and a typical functional or product-based structure. As they grow to maturity, organisations tend to drift towards formality and control from the centre, including standardisation of operating procedures, policies to govern many aspects of what they do, and more formal processes for managing their staff. However, taking on the trappings of maturity also means that organisations are naturally less adaptive to changes in the environment.

Organisations tend to get into difficulty with change, for different reasons at various stages of their growth. In infancy or as developing businesses, they frequently get into trouble through poor internal controls, overtrading or weak management. More mature organisations, however, because of their inability to adapt easily to the changing circumstances, are more vulnerable to turbulence and rapid changes in the environment. In recent years, this has been reflected in public utilities such as RTÉ and the ESB, along with mature private-sector companies like Waterford Crystal and Guinness, having to wrestle with change and transformation.

DEGREE OF CHANGE

The basic definitions of change have been amended in recent years to distinguish between first-order or incremental change and second-order change, variously called frame breaking or discontinuous change. Most organisations today acknowledge the need for incremental change, and many have introduced continuous improvement programmes (CIP) as a way of embedding change in the culture. However, in the current circumstances, that level of change is generally insufficient to meet the needs of a rapidly changing environment. Data from the survey suggests that managers who claim that their organisations are changing all the time often fail to recognise the distinction between first- and second-order change and the need for major periodic re-alignments as well as continuous improvement.

> If you are not changing, you are standing still. If you don't have continuous change, you can easily fall behind and require much more radical change. This is a more difficult form of change to manage if you haven't been doing the other stuff.

PROGRAMMED AND PROCESS APPROACHES TO CHANGE

In the past number of years, there has been growing criticism of the failure of many change programmes to achieve the results that they intended. Until recently, the prevailing management mind-set has been to view change as a project or a programme to be implemented in a systematic way in response to externally driven demands for new technology or systems, and for improved quality, service, and delivery. Not only have a variety of programmed approaches such as Business Process Re-engineering, Customer Relationship Management, Performance Management, and TQM provided a convenient label for senior management to sell change to the workforce, but they have also been strongly marketed by consulting companies who find it much easier to sell product than process.

> Ideas and strategies are important, of course, but execution is the real challenge.

> — PERCY BARNEVIK (FORMER CEO OF ABB)

In response to a growing scepticism about the benefits of programmed approaches to change, there is increasing awareness in many Irish organisations that change management is not a recipe for implementing new strategies, systems, technology or structures, but essentially a re-educative process for getting staff at all levels to take ownership for making those changes work. Traditional approaches to change, which included announcing change from the top, using consultants to sell change or negotiating for change, have given way to more inclusive approaches where staff are involved from the start in the planning and implementation process. This changing management mind-set has coincided with a realisation by many organisations that their most sustainable competitive advantage is developing a culture that allows them to adapt quickly to external events, and that change is not so much about managing specific events as about creating a self-renewing or learning organisation.

2.3 TYPES OF CHANGE EFFORT

Most of the managers surveyed for this report identified their organisations as experiencing significant external forces for change and felt that they were making substantial responses. While the data suggests that the main focus of change is on restructuring, upgrading technology and introducing new strategies, it is worth observing that these are often vehicles for matching the competition and responding to customer demands for improved service, quality or product range. As elaborated later in this briefing, most change efforts are ultimately designed to change the culture of the organisation, so that it is in a better position to respond to the future demands of major stakeholders, whether customers, staff or suppliers.

Types of Change Effort	
Type	**% reported**
New structures/restructuring	46
New or upgraded technology	43
Strategic shift — e.g. developing new markets	35
Changes in work practices — e.g. teamwork	24
Introduction of new systems — e.g. MRP, performance management	20
Mergers/acquisitions	17

Selected comments from respondents on their current change process include the following:

- We are changing individual roles and reporting relationships to create more flexibility and teamwork — it is driven by client needs.

- We are working at upgrading the technology to allow the company to provide placement services on the Internet.

- We are upgrading our software every three weeks and our hardware every eight months.

- We are undergoing major changes under two umbrella programmes — "Go to Market", designed to realign our sales force with the changing needs of the customer; and "Change for Growth", an effort to redesign our infrastructure.

- We are refocusing our teams in corporate banking with a great deal of moving around of personnel and a redefinition of team roles.

2.4 Initiators of Change

Although the question of who or what drives change internally is necessarily subjective (where you stand is what you see), there is little doubt from the survey that, although a great deal of successful change is managed through the middle levels, it is led mainly by senior management. While the roles of senior management or individual leaders at the top are usually more clearly defined if the organisation has gone through a merger or is facing into an obvious crisis, one of the main functions of top management is to create a sense of urgency for change. Sometimes that is achieved through inspiring people with a vision for the future, and sometimes by dramatising the problems so that a "burning platform" is presented, where there is little option but to change.

GREENFIELD CHANGE AT THE EQUALITY INVESTIGATIONS AGENCY

Although the Equality Investigations Agency is a relatively new organisation, it is taking on functions that were previously shared by the Equality Agency and the Labour Relations Commission. It has also inherited a number of their staff. While the agency has a clear mandate to deal with cases of discrimination on nine grounds, and has the force of the Equal Status Act, the challenge, according to the director, is "setting up the new agency while at the same time trying to change it".

Although some staff members are new or volunteers, others were assigned to the agency and there has been a degree of cynicism to overcome in getting buy-in to the new organisation. Some success has been achieved through agreeing a mission statement, clarifying four core principles or values, and instituting regular meetings with the staff. But there is still a considerable task ahead in creating a service where everyone shares the need for customer service and timely adjudication on equality issues.

While there is work to be done in attracting people to avail of the service, the real challenge for the director is to determine how to cascade the mission down through the staff and to introduce suitable performance-management systems to develop and sustain the mission. While each of the equality officers remains independent on specific cases, there is also a need to integrate the organisation so that the information and knowledge held by each person is shared at a professional level and that staff take ownership of the overarching goals of the agency to develop a professional, robust, accessible and timely service.

Over 60 per cent of respondents in the survey identified their change process as led from the top, and 40 per cent identified an individual leader as key to the success of the process. A leader with a vision was seen as critical in three of the five in-depth case studies conducted for this briefing, while in two cases a group of managers below senior level was seen as providing much of the energy and time for the process. It reflects the importance in most change efforts of direction and leadership from the top (a guiding coalition), synergy between the top and the middles, and a critical mass of managers and key staff at all levels to facilitate the process while others keep the organisation afloat.

- The director is the driver — her style is very inclusive — we had weekly meetings of all the staff so that everyone would take ownership of the vision.

- The senior managers made time and space for the change. We pulled fifty-seven people out of the business to manage it while the others kept the business going — we took the hit.

- He presented the business with a challenge to double sales in five years and the company brought in new managers with a ruthless commitment to getting results.

INITIATORS AND FACILITATORS OF CHANGE	% responses
Senior management group	61
A change leader/champion at the top	40
Middle management group	14
Specialist staff HR/OD/IT/ consultants	10
A specific group of managers	9

2.5 THE CHANGE PROCESS

Change theory still relies fairly heavily on the work of Kurt Lewin who suggested three stages in any change process: unfreezing, change and refreezing (often called Readiness, Transition, and Institutionalisation).[1] Although some commentators suggest that many organisations today exist in conditions of constant change where there are no distinct stages in the process, as indicated earlier, these models are not mutually exclusive.

While most Irish managers are experiencing ongoing change in their organisations, much of it is incremental, and that level of change is normally managed through the existing structures or through continuous improvement processes (CIP). However, most managers also recognise that, while having mechanisms for dealing with incremental change makes it easier to make periodic major re-alignments, each change requires: a readiness process to ensure that staff are actively committed; a transition process to move things forward; and a process to bed down the changes as part of the culture.

Many change programmes founder on the rocks of lack of buy-in by those responsible for ensuring the success of the change effort, while others run out of energy before the real benefits of the process have time to emerge. Yet others fail to realise the benefits they promised because insufficient attention is paid to integrating the new systems or work practices into a culture that traditionally supported and rewarded other behaviours and norms. Not only have many Irish organisations had to deal with a legacy of badly managed change that involved decree, negotiation and compensation for change, but many managers have yet to learn the skills for dealing with transition as a messy and serendipitous process rather than a rational or systematic programme.

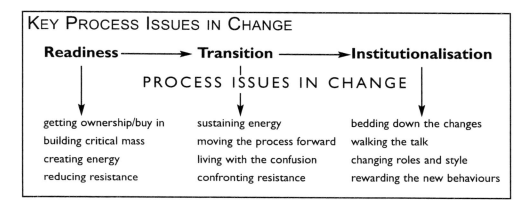

Although many are at an early stage of the learning curve with change, there are encouraging signs from the survey and interview data to suggest that increasing numbers of Irish organisations have recognised that change requires skilful management if it is to achieve real and lasting benefits. Also reflected in the data are indications that Irish organisations are becoming increasingly aware that, in the long term, most change is about realigning people to new roles and relationships, getting staff to work better with each other, and developing closer ties with customers and suppliers. Waterford Crystal and ESB Powergen are examples of organisations that have learned through a number of less than successful turnaround attempts that the only sustainable way to manage in a global economy is to create a culture that includes involvement, information sharing and empowerment at all levels.

2.6 STAGES IN THE PROCESS

While 43 per cent of respondents in the survey reported their organisations as being halfway through a change effort, it is important to caution that organisations and managers are inclined to undervalue the need for readiness and to push too rapidly into transition, which often leads to lack of ownership and resistance down the line. In organisations where there has been a history of failed attempts at change or lack of trust, there is usually a need to slow the readiness process down sufficiently so that those affected or who need to be on board with the process are convinced. However, the critical obstacle to many change efforts reported from the survey is not lack of trust or vision, but insufficient time and other resources being dedicated to the change. Some organisations divert a great deal of management time to their change process. Irish Life, for example, seconded a large number of staff to change project teams. Others, like a division of ITG, schedule time for change meetings in the same way as time for operational meetings.

By and large, organisations embark on change not because they want to, but because they have to in order to stay healthy and avoid decline. This chapter has examined the external driving forces and the internal responses to change in Irish organisations. Most organisations, over time, develop the skills to manage incremental growth, which has traditionally been sufficient to facilitate their evolution towards maturity. However, in conditions of turbulence and accelerated change, as witnessed in Ireland over the past decade, most organisations must also learn new strategies and skills for dealing with the current level and speed of change.

Furthermore, while there are indications from the interview and survey data that many companies have developed new mind-sets and skills around continuous and discontinuous changes, it is apparent that others have yet to be convinced of the alternatives to programmed or turnaround responses. The pathology of organisations that have managed painful transitions or been rescued from decline has gone some way to educate managers on the need to develop a capacity to make rapid adjustments to the environment. However, other managers have yet to learn that, in today's conditions, you either anticipate and manage change or you wait for the inevitable crisis that will force you to change in ways that may limit your options.

3

CRITICAL SUCCESS FACTORS IN CHANGE

Over the past decade, a great deal of the commentary on organisational change has been anecdotal and hindsight, tending to highlight the successes and minimise the failures. It prompted Phil Murvis some years ago to publish a book called *Failures in Organisation Development and Change*[1] to balance the reported successes against the many process failures in change. At this stage, however, most Irish managers have their own experiences of change from one, and sometimes several, organisations, creating a rich vein of data on the success factors, the major blocks to change and the lessons they have learned from those experiences. This chapter seeks to report on and explore the key success factors in change.

3.1 KEY SUCCESS FACTORS

In recent years, several writers, like Kotter[2] and Beer,[3] have suggested lists of key success factors in change efforts, which in some respects are not too dissimilar to the findings in this briefing. However, because of the size of Irish organisations and their relative stage of growth, the data from this study provides a richer insight than the data from studies based on large mature US corporations. The findings indicate that the key characteristics of successful change in Irish organisations are as follows:

CRITICAL FACTORS IN SUCCESSFUL CHANGE (RANK ORDER)
1. Leadership at the top and management in the middle
2. Quality communication at all levels
3. A shared vision and clear objectives for the change
4. Having the key clients on board with the change
5. A detailed and evolving planning process
6. Middle management buy-in to the change effort
7. A critical mass of support at all levels
8. Time and other resources dedicated to the process

---

1. LEADERSHIP AT THE TOP AND MANAGEMENT IN THE MIDDLE

While it is generally accepted that most successful change efforts are led from the top, there is evidence that many are, in fact, driven by the "middles" — the guiding coalition that Kotter[4] identifies as key to most successful transformations is usually a mix of senior and middle managers. As many Irish organisations introduce flatter structures and become differentiated by technology, product or customer, it is more likely that even strategic changes will be driven by groups of middle managers. This has been the case with ITG, which has restructured into separate business units, each division managing its own transition.

Assessing the impact and contribution of top leadership to successful change is difficult for a number of reasons. Firstly, it is often easier to define leadership when it is absent than when it is present. While managers often identify with a lack of leadership, it is difficult to say what leaders really do in times of change. Critics of some of the more popular accounts of organisational transformations have suggested that, after successful change efforts, leaders often have attributed to them qualities that would not have been attributed had the change been a failure. Moreover, change leadership has tended to be associated with the qualities of the person at the top rather than with the process, and has been overly identified with "heroic" leaders who rescue companies in crisis, rather than with leaders who manage healthy transitions.

Some commentators and researchers make a distinction between transactional leadership, where leaders use incentives and rewards to gain acceptance for the system's strategies, the norms and behaviours they want to encourage, and transformational leadership, where the leader creates a vision, excites people about the journey and empowers followers to see beyond the existing paradigm. The suggestion is that transactional leadership is more appropriate to first-order change where the focus is on improving existing practices, and transformational leadership more appropriate where there is a need to replace the existing business model, radically realign the organisation, or merge two cultures. In those conditions, the role of leadership is to create a crisis that leaves little option but for the organisation to change, to inspire people with a compelling vision, and to instil confidence at all levels.

In three of the case studies for this briefing, top leadership was seen as providing a significant impetus to the change effort in signalling a new beginning, importing a new business model, re-focusing the organisation, and creating a shared vision for the future. Interestingly, several consultants identified with a similar quality at the top, as the "courage" to articulate a vision for change when there was no obvious crisis and to persist through the con-fusion, anger and resistance that accompanies the process. Also associated with top leadership courage was the need to tackle senior people who had a vested interest in the status quo or lacked the ability to hack the new vision, particularly if they had been personal friends or had a long history with the company.

The Role of Leadership in Change

- Creating a compelling vision or dramatising the crisis

- Energising the staff/shareholders/customers for the process

- Focusing people on the longer-term needs of the business

- Developing and declaring a new strategic intent/long-term objectives

- Acting as a standard bearer or champion for the process

- Encouraging and recognising people's effort and results

However, although leadership is generally associated with senior management, Kotter also suggests that, in times of change, you require leadership at all levels — "you can't manage people into battle". An apparent paradox in the literature on change is that, while acknowledging middle management as a key factor in most successful transitions, middle managers are also seen as one of the chief obstacles to change. Not only have many commentators on change tended to embellish the qualities of top leaders, but they have also been inclined to discount the role of the "middles" in implementing and supporting change at lower levels.

Frohman and Johnson in *The Middle Management Challenge*[5] conclude that the "middles" are often sidelined by senior managers going directly to the staff with proposals for change. However, Michael Beer, from six case studies, found that, in five of them, change was primarily led by middle managers rather than from the top. Not only does this survey and other research by the author suggest that middle managers are important in implementing change, but the findings also imply that senior managers identify some middle managers as critical to the success of the process.

2. QUALITY COMMUNICATIONS AT ALL LEVELS

A second critical factor in successful change is communications. At one level, communications is seen as vital in getting people on board with the need for change; at another level it is seen as necessary in engaging people during the process so that they remain committed to making the change work.

Getting the key people on board is critical at the start of any process, and assuming that the staff understand and share the need for change is one of the chief reasons for resistance. Marvin Weisbord, in the book *Productive Workplaces*,[6] talks of getting all the actors under one roof so that they can share the need and direction of the change, while Jack Welch, ex-president, puts it more succinctly: "When everyone has the same information, they generally reach the same conclusion."[7]

A second and no less important reason for improving the quality of communications during any change process is to foster involvement and ownership. Most Irish organisations have learned in the past decade that top-down changes like restructuring or new technology will only work if those affected are involved in the planning and implementation process. In relation to getting key people on board with any change, their involvement in identifying the key issues and planning for the future is often vital to convincing them that the degree of change being proposed is necessary.

Part of any communications process in change also involves the active participation of key staff in generating and making sense of the data that relates to where the organisation is going for the future, and in agreeing new measures of success. Organisations often measure the things they can measure rather than the things that they want to change, and involving staff in the process of measuring the sometimes difficult and softer areas of the business, such as customer service or cost of service, is important for getting them on board and energised about making change happen.

> Research showed that Waterford was not delivering the right products at the right price — data also showed that people didn't associate Waterford Crystal with Ireland.

When organisations have been through painful or unsuccessful changes in the past and there is emotional baggage from those incidents, communications is also a vital part of the process for re-establishing the trust needed for change to be managed without resistance. Lack of trust is a major barrier to change and part of the process is often to surface and deal with un-resolved issues before people are willing to come on board in a positive way. While some organisations, aware that there are issues of trust, use external consultants to provide a more even-handed and skilful approach to convincing people of the need for change, others recognise that creating readiness means making time to share information, listen to people's concerns and educate staff in the business process as a way of acknowledging the need for a qualitative improvement in communications.

> Trust is a big issue. It is in danger of killing the change. Eighty-five per cent of our staff are in denial; they think they are shielded by the customer and their letters of comfort.

TOOLS FOR IMPROVING INTERNAL COMMUNICATIONS

- Regular staff meetings
- Cross-functional teams/task groups
- Culture and climate surveys
- Mentoring
- Team briefing
- Ideas boxes
- Programmes – ISO/Q Mark
- Open book accounting
- Climate/culture surveys
- Pocket reminders
- Job rotation
- 360-degree appraisal
- Off sites
- Task groups/implementation
- Public goal setting and review

- Bi-annual presentations to all staff
- Weekly questions and answers
- House journals
- Renewal conferences
- E-mail shots
- Info share/intranet
- Skip level meetings
- Benchmark visits
- Update meetings
- Vision/values teams
- Quality circles
- Interpersonal skills training
- Team building
- Team Leadership training
- Vision/values project groups

However, while communications is seen as an important vehicle in creating readiness for change, it is also critical to implementation. Many organisations have strengthened their internal communications processes as part of an overall strategy for sharing their vision and values, for involving staff in continuous improvement, for creating more flexibility for change and for building a climate where there are no surprises. While not all communications initiatives are related to change, many of them are a response to an environment that suggests the need for more flexibility, adaptability, faster response time and the creation of new organisational structures that reflect the changing circumstances.

3. A SHARED VISION AND CLEAR OBJECTIVES FOR THE CHANGE

It is generally acknowledged that there are only two real drivers for change — an impending crisis (burning platform), or a compelling vision for the future.

A shared vision for the change is critical to most processes. Firstly, it provides a sense of direction for the future — "Where will we be at the end of this process that is a better place where we are now?" While a shared vision helps to provide a rationale for change, it also helps to generate energy for the journey and a challenge to succeed — the reason why many organisations define their vision in the form of a strategic intent (long-term targets or goals). While successive change efforts at Waterford Crystal have been driven by the challenge to double sales — "Waterford 250" and "Waterford 500" the current strategic intent at Irish Life is to reduce the cost of doing business from 2 per cent to 1 per cent in preparation for a "one per cent world".

Secondly, a shared vision serves a purpose in providing some certainty in what can otherwise be an anxious and uncertain journey into the future. Moreover, while taking time to clarify and communicate a vision for the change provides a shared sense of where the organisation is going, redefining the values as part of that process acts as "organisational glue", helping people at all levels to recognise what they are trying to preserve and the inspiration for getting there.

> It has taken some time to get our demands together. We have had to change our culture to include services in other areas, also to engender a culture of speed so that people aren't kept waiting. Our four guiding principles include professionalism, robustness, accessibility and timeliness.

Thirdly, clarifying and sharing a strategic intent or vision for the change provides a logical starting point for any change process, creating a broad sense of direction, from which objectives, goals, projects and action plans can cascade down through the organisation. Several consultants also emphasised the need for a detailed vision and hard detail on the process, with rigorous drivers and milestones for every stage of the journey — described by one consultant as a "War Office" approach. Not only does having a detailed plan help the various stakeholders identify with the need for change, but it also shows where their contribution fits into the broader strategy. Furthermore, in an organisation with a history of continuous success, the creation of a new strategic intent can also be a way of weaning people away from the complacency of doing more of the same and help to realign them with the future needs of a more competitive and demanding environment.

It was a different level of change — change before was obvious.

4. HAVING THE KEY CLIENTS ON BOARD

Sometimes described as the internal clients for change, the key people in any change process are defined by two simple questions — "Who needs to be on board with this change for it to be successful?" and "Who could stop it from happening?" In any process, there are key individuals, strategic groups and sometimes whole levels of the organisation that are key to successful implementation.

While, ideally, everyone needs to be committed to change, the notion of a "critical mass" suggests that you don't need everyone on board, but you do need enough key individuals and groups actively supporting a change effort for it to be successful. Moreover, while there are those who need to support and become actively involved in the process, it is also important to recognise the role of those who are passive or even resistant to the change. They also play a part in slowing down the change enough to prevent those who may be less thoughtful from rushing into a process that may meet resistance down the line. Also, during any change process, there is always a need for people to run the day-to-day business while others are more actively involved and focused on the change. Research suggests that there is a need for change managers and non-change managers and that both are key to successful transition.

Apart from identifying those who need to be actively involved and those who are likely to be less involved in a change process, there are implications for educating and training staff. While, in today's environment, all levels need to be educated for change so that they understand the rational frameworks and human processes involved, it is also important to identify the cadre of key people who will be more actively involved, and to provide them with opportunities to develop the knowledge and skills for facilitating and managing change.

Merger at Irish Life

Transforming Irish Life from a semi-state organisation to a commercial entity has not been without pain. However, it has seen the emergence of a renewed organisation that is now firmly in the financial services sector, with new products and a network to deliver them.

In 1993, realising that its cost base was too high, the company went through a 20 per cent reduction in headcount, which it soon realised was not enough to stem the decline. Following a series of incremental cost-cutting exercises and a costly strike by the sales force, there was clearly a need for more radical change. With new chief executive, David Went, and the senior team providing leadership, and the recognition that a commercial focus could not be achieved through incremental change, Irish Life entered into a merger with the Irish Permanent.

Bringing together the systems and structures from both companies was achieved over an eight-month period by pulling sixty staff out for twelve weeks so that business could continue while the changes were made — "You have to create space and worry about the impact afterwards." The group worked in teams of six, each with a project leader and a sponsor, working on twelve business streams and 57 design issues to achieve the "best of the best" from each company. Thirty staff continued working on implementation for a further year.

Part of the merger process involved managers reapplying for their own jobs, which not only ensured fairness in choosing the best talent from both companies but also destabilised things sufficiently for the change to take place — "a very maturing process", according to one senior manager. The process also involved a great deal of talking with staff, getting their concerns out into the open, not only to allay cynicism but also to keep communications channels open between management and staff — "It's hard to hate someone you are seeing every week."

While the merger was swift, there is still a long way to go. Success at bringing the structures and systems together has now to be matched by merging the cultures, particularly in the middle, if they are to achieve the benefits of a full integration and meet the demands of the consumer and the competition. With the growth in low-cost providers and a move to direct selling, retaining market share means that the company will not only have to grow by 80 per cent in the next three years but, if it is to survive in a "one per cent world", will also have to reduce its costs of doing business from 2 per cent to 1 per cent.

5. A DETAILED PLANNING PROCESS

Some years ago, in a presentation on change, Tom Roche, then Chairman of CRH, suggested that there are only two ingredients in any change process — "planning and communications". While these elements are, to some extent, linked, they also represent a practical dichotomy for managers around whether a change should be planned in detail or should be a more evolving process.

One of the contending issues in change is that, while people want the certainty of a detailed plan, the reality is that change is usually less certain and sequential than represented by GANT charts or project schedulers. Also, while change, by its very nature, implies uncertainty, for real change to take place it is necessary that people are anxious and confused and learn to live with a degree of instability over the period of the transition. Even in the literature on change there is some theoretical debate on the merits of the Planned Change versus the Action Research model as they apply to managed change. Lack of planning can undermine a change process, but so too can a programmed approach, where sticking to the plan or meeting the project deadlines becomes more important than managing the process issues that can ultimately bedevil the implementation.

What is most apparent from the case studies and the view of the consultants is the criticality of creating robust structures for change and the need to make time for planning, implementation and review. Making time to manage the process is ranked eighth in the list of success factors for change, illustrated by the Irish Life experience where sixty staff-members were pulled out of the business to create time and space for planning. Meanwhile, as part of its transformation from a product- to a results-driven business, Waterford Crystal also put a great deal of energy into re-clarifying management roles and setting up a cross-functional team to work on its vision and values. ESB Powergen established a full-time change team of six staff to facilitate the power stations managing their own transition processes. Several consultants also identified with the need for senior management to be seen to walk the talk by making resources available, and to manage the energy level by not overloading their staff with projects that could lead to change burnout — "You can't bolt change onto someone's existing job when they are already under pressure.'

3.2 APPROACHES AND TOOLS IN CHANGE

There is a certain predictability about the tools and approaches that organisations use to bring about change. The changing fads reported by Pascale, in *Managing on the Edge*,[8] as having currency at particular times — such as MBO, strategic business units (SBUs), MRP, Teambuilding, BPR, CRM, TQM or quality circles — may have had something to do with what training organisations and consultants were promoting at the time. However, many of the techniques or programmes used in organisations to promote change are often selected because they are tangible and easy to sell. In any event, organisations do make use of a variety of packaged tools in support of their change processes, some tailoring them to their own requirements and others using consultants to provide more objective and skilful facilitation of the process.

More fundamental, however, than the fads and programmes used to facilitate change are the tasks that organisations use to drive the process. Although it is essentially the process issues that are being managed in any change effort, it is tasks and projects that drive process, which range from off sites and task groups to celebrations and a variety of techniques for sharing information and measuring the benefits of change.

TASK GROUPS

One of the most popular tools in organisational change is setting up task groups and implementation teams to generate and share data, to manage the implementation of agreed actions or as a support mechanism during change. As in many companies where team meetings are a common feature of the business process, so managers and staff have also become more comfortable with being assigned to temporary groups as a feature in change.

For task groups to be effective, they should generally be fairly small — some 6–8 people; have a senior management sponsor; have a limited life, meet regularly; have clear terms of reference; receive training; and report to some form of plenary group. Within a change process, task groups also have several more covert functions. Originally reported from field experiments that were designed to encourage housewives to consider alternative food sources during the Second World War, discussion groups have proven to be one of the most effective ways of changing attitudes. Furthermore, while task groups and project teams serve a process function in changing mind-sets and attitudes, they are also part of the machinery for managing instability during a transition. Change inevitably creates uncertainty and confusion about the future, and task groups serve the purpose of helping to create that instability while also providing a mechanism to harness uncertainty for the positive benefit of the process.

Task groups require careful managing with clear terms of reference, models and frameworks for pulling together their findings, a process for reporting back and mechanisms for integrating their efforts into the overall planning process. As a rule, task groups do not make decisions but focus on an aspect of the process by generating and sharing data, suggesting options and assisting others in making decisions based on the emerging consensus. That process needs to be facilitated in such a way that groups do not arrive at quick and simplistic solutions to complex issues and then expect others to deliver on them without question.

TRAINING AND DEVELOPMENT

Training is still one of the most popular and cost-effective tools in change. At more senior levels, various external development and education programmes — such as executive MBAs or senior management workshops — are often used to shift managers' thinking from their current mind-set and expose them to new business models and frameworks. Another tried and tested way of helping managers to develop their ideas and challenge their own thinking is to expose them to what is being done in other companies through plant visits or benchmarking exercises.

As an alternative to bringing in new blood, some companies have begun to use internal assessment centres and non-traditional programmes, such as outdoors training, management-style audits, sensitivity labs, competency profiling and professional mentoring. It is clear that, in recent years, training has broadened in scope away from the purely functional aspects of the person's job, towards helping staff and managers develop broader skills in areas like coaching, group facilitation, business literacy, and change project management. Moreover, as one of the co-authors of *Funky Business*[9] suggested in a recent interview, many organisations are now beginning to recruit people for their attitudes, energy and values, and to train them in specific job skills, rather than the other way around.

Also included under the heading of 'training as a tool in change' is assigning managers to the process, as internal change agents. While 44 per cent of survey respondents indicated that staff-members were trained in change management, there are very few public programmes on offer in Ireland or abroad. Although some training is supplied by consultants or may form part of an executive development programme, many managers seem to learn their change-management skills through being in organisations where change is the norm. It appears that the main avenue for managers to develop skills for handling change is their experience with change itself. This supports previous research findings by the author that it is mainly destabilising career events that help managers to develop the confidence they need to take charge of change in their own areas.

MEASURABLE TARGETS AND TRACKING

In the past few years, several writers have built on the ground-breaking research of Locke and Latham which showed fairly conclusively that challenging goals and feedback provide the greatest motivation to performance improvement. One of the major lessons from the quality movement, and one that is spelled out in detail by Edward Deming in his seminal work on quality improvement, was the need to set clear standards and challenging targets and to track their achievement publicly. At a more strategic level, others, like Gary Hamel, have promoted the idea of a vision for change expressed as a measurable strategic intent, while the concept of HAGs (Hairy Audacious Goals) identified by Poras and Collins[10] as a feature of the more resilient companies has gained some popularity in creating and energising measurable challenges for change.

Although they have become part of the public image for some organisations, one of the reasons why measurable targets and

---

MAJOR TOOLS AND TECHNIQUES IN CHANGE (RANK ORDER)

1. Setting up task groups and project teams
2. Training in new approaches and skills training
3. Identifying measurable targets, tracking and publicising them
4. Use of external consultants to facilitate part of the process
5. Having a transition team to manage the overall process
6. Training in change management
7. Changing the rewards system

tracking have been slow to emerge as a common feature in change is that they don't so easily apply to the qualitative things that many organisations are trying to improve, such as customer service, client care, and integration. Furthermore, most overarching goals or strategic intent tend to be expressed in output terms, which ignores many of the intervening challenges along the way, such as creating better teamwork, improving communications or changing management style. Setting a target to increase output by 50 per cent in three years or reduce delivery time to 24 hours is fine if there is also a process to make it happen, which deals with the need to radically improve performance in some of the softer areas like style, attitudes, interpersonal skills, quality, value and teamwork.

While in two of the five case-study examples stretch goals were used to energise the process, other organisations used public awards as targets for change — ISO, Quality Mark or Excellence through People, for example. Moreover, although under 6 per cent of the survey respondents acknowledged questionnaires and surveys as part of their change process, internal and external culture and climate surveys (including quality or service audits) have increasingly become benchmarks for measuring improvement in organisations.

USE OF EXTERNAL CONSULTANTS

Some 57 per cent of questionnaire respondents in the survey indicated that their organisations had used external consultants to help manage a recent change, their main role being to convince the staff of the need for change. Consultants have traditionally been used by companies to deliver an expert or objective view, and several major criticisms of consultants include their tendency to find what they predict and to leave the company with recommendations but little shared ownership for implementation.

However, in the past decade, there have been moves by many Irish companies to use consultants to front-end the change process, whether by doing an initial diagnosis, carrying out survey feedback, facilitating workshops or off sites and, in some cases, helping to manage the complete process. Also, compared with even a decade ago, there are more consultants with good process skills, many of whom have learned their craft by having been in OD or HRM departments of organisations that have experienced a great deal of change, or by shadowing external consultants as internal counterparts.

A TRANSITION TEAM TO MANAGE THE PROCESS

Fairly well established as a key element in change management is the notion that the traditional organisation structures are best suited to handling the operational side of the business, but less effective at managing change. Any significant change process demands a new set of skills and a different mind-set from that of running the business. It also requires the setting up of additional structures, sometimes called "shadow organisation". Depending on the process, shadow organisation may include a transition team, task groups, cluster groups, steering committees, project owners, audit teams, briefing groups, workouts, implementation groups and other aspects of structure specific to organisational change.

One of the design elements in change is a transition team, whose function is to provide overall management of the process while others get on with running the business. In most cases, a transition team does not require full-time dedicated staff, as with the ESB or Irish Life, but it does require regular meetings to design, implement and review the process.

While transition teams usually include representatives of top management, they also include middle managers and sometimes a diagonal slice of staff and an external consultant. They normally comprise fewer than ten people, and critical to selection is identifying individuals with an understanding of the complexities of change, a potential for developing process skills, energy and a willingness to commit their time. Moreover, if the change process takes place over a lengthy period, membership of the team may be rotated as a way of developing key staff, committing managers to the process and producing a stream of internal consultants who can be used whenever there is a need for process or facilitation skills.

REFOCUSING THE REWARDS SYSTEM

One significant tool for institutionalising new behaviours and attitudes in support of change is modifying the rewards system to focus on the things the organisation is trying to encourage — "What you reward is what you get." If, as an organisation, you are trying to encourage quality and yet the organisation is rewarding people for output, the result may be high wastage, rework and customer complaints. In Waterford Crystal, as part of the process for moving towards a results-based culture, the company detailed individual roles, including measured accountabilities for each employee, and introduced a new bonusing system, 40 per cent of which is related to meeting personal objectives.

Not only is changing the rewards system an output variable in some change efforts, but it is often a vital constituent in the process. As an incentive to involvement, reward can take on many forms — such as the celebration of milestones in the process, involving people in task groups, external benchmarking exercises, making presentations, attending training courses or conferences, and being consulted about the change, whether through surveys, interviews or group discussions.

This chapter confirms that a considerable amount of learning has taken place in Irish organisations over the past decade on the management of change. It suggests that many organisations have moved away from a mind-set of implementing change through decree, negotiation or expert consultants, in the direction of more inclusive and participative approaches. It also confirms that Irish managers are more familiar with change, having experienced turnaround, transition and transformation in two, and sometimes three companies, and as a result have developed confidence and skills in change management. The findings also suggest that managers are more aware of the process side of change and are more willing to acknowledge that it takes time, a great deal of planning and increased communications at all levels.

However, while there has been a signal shift in the mind-set of many Irish managers and organisations, it has to be viewed as part of a landscape where many organisations still rely heavily on negotiation as a primary strategy in change, and the recent history of some Irish companies still reflects the use of turnaround strategies and last-minute agreements. In addition, over-reaction by some companies to the events of 11 September 2001, including immediate lay-offs and hurried retrenchments, tends to suggest that some companies are using external events as a spurious rationale for dealing with issues that they should have confronted and dealt with in the past.

4

THE MAIN BLOCKS TO CHANGE

Apart from examining the critical success factors in change, there are also insights to be gained from examining the conditions that prevent change from taking place — as some commentators suggest, "If there were no obstacles to change, it would be simple enough to announce it." In the 1960s and 1970s, many changes in Irish organisations were top-down and by decree; this resulted in a considerable amount of resistance in the form of strikes, mistrust of management and a legacy of negotiated change that has lasted to this day. What has most influenced the management mind-set on change over the past decade has been the environment, which demands a more motivated, flexible and adaptive workforce, and where customer service, quality and innovation have become major competitive advantages. These things cannot be achieved as easily through compliance, threats or negotiation.

However, although Irish organisations have become more enlightened in their approach to change, there are still many unanticipated blocks that persist, suggesting that there is room for organisational learning and more thoughtful approaches to change management. While the major blocks to change confirmed by the survey are listed below, as some of them overlap, they are combined into broad categories.

MAIN BLOCKS TO CHANGE
1. Insufficient buy-in and ownership
   — Lack of commitment from the top
   — Lack of middle-management ownership
   — Insufficient support at all levels
2. Unrealistic timescale for change
   — Loss of energy
   — Lack of resources

> 3. Lack of trust
>   — Failed attempts at change
>   — Lack of vision or a process
>   — Inadequate internal communications
> 4. Lack of readiness for change
>   — Problems with letting go
>   — Overt and covert resistance

4.1 Insufficient Buy-in and Ownership

The findings of this study confirm a major conclusion from the Arthur D. Little study where lack of buy-in from managers and staff was identified as the most daunting obstacle to change, with over 64 per cent of respondents recognising it as the most serious blockage.[1]

As a block to change, lack of ownership is often recognised only some time into a change process, because at the start it is not anticipated. While programmes such as TQM or ISO are often sold to employees by consultants and trainers as a panacea for quality or service improvement, and organisational restructurings are announced with appropriate fanfare by senior management, so in other change efforts a hand show of support for change is often mistakenly taken as buy-in from the staff. The survey respondents for this briefing identified lack of ownership in three distinct areas: lack of commitment from the top; lack of middle-management support; and insufficient support for the process, at all levels.

Lack of Commitment from the Top

While the survey findings identified leadership as a critical element in most successful change efforts, the existing leadership is some-times one of the main obstacles to change. Apart from the fact that senior managers frequently have the most to lose, their thinking is often blocked by the very mind-set that needs to change if the transition is to be successful. Moreover, as comments from the survey also suggest, senior managers often lack the mental models or conceptual skills to manage transition in any way other than they have in the past.

While some organisations deal with lack of top management commitment by replacement or restructuring (Irish Life as part of its process insisted that all managers re-apply for their own jobs), or bring in new blood at the top (Waterford Crystal), others recognise that commitment to change means senior managers making time to plan and communicate a vision for the future, skilfully manage the transition process and lead by example.

> There is a lack of ownership at all levels, among managers as well as the workforce. There is a storm coming and no sense of a vision for the future — there is a real lack of walking the talk from the top.

LACK OF MIDDLE-MANAGEMENT OWNERSHIP

While middle managers are often seen as a bridge between the vision at the top and specific changes lower down, lack of buy-in by the "middles" can also be a serious blockage to implementation.

> Middle managers — they can be the greatest enabler or the biggest blockage to change.

There are several reasons why middle managers are often seen as a major block to change. Firstly, they are frequently ignored or by-passed in programmed approaches to change, which are planned and announced by top management. In the process, middle managers are often not directly involved until they are identified as an obstacle to implementation. Also, middle managers have traditionally exercised a control function in organisations — a bridge between management decision-making and orderly execution. Change processes that are designed to empower staff at lower levels tend to undermine the traditional control function of the middles, and as such middle managers often have most to lose.

Finally, in many change efforts, middle managers are not brought into the planning process early enough, while the expectation at the top is that they will be a key element in implementation. The end result is that middle managers are often expected to implement what they had little hand in creating and to defend what they don't understand — and, as Ron Lippitt once suggested, "When people don't understand what is going on, the easiest thing is to be obstructionist."

> The managers (middle) were so traumatised by the process that they abandoned the staff. They ran around saying, "I don't know what is happening — I am as confused as you are."

While some organisations have followed the fashion of dealing with middle management resistance by removing individuals or whole levels from the organisation, others have embarked on programmes to re-educate their middle managers to take on new roles and to involve them early on as a key group in the planning and implementation process.

- We were overmanned in 1996 so we found those who were interested and capable and, through voluntary severance, began working with a new cohort in the middle — we educated them about change, made them smarter managers. Having been through the process once, they are less fearful and more mature in relation to change.

- The middle managers have become so institutionalised in industrial relations — in the win–lose approach. They haven't been sold on the concept of competitive advantage through people.

- We tried to implement a revised business model a few years ago. The plan was ill thought through. Trust broke down and the lack of middle-management support eventually led to the project being abandoned.

INSUFFICIENT SUPPORT AT ALL LEVELS

The concept of "critical mass" suggests that, although you don't need everyone on board for change to be successful, you do need enough people to balance the inevitable resistance that accompanies transition. Lack of critical mass for change often results in the process getting dragged down by the negative energy of the complacent, the obstructionists and the terrorists.

While critical mass is partly a question of the numbers of people supporting a change effort, it is more precisely defined by the extent to which the key clients have ownership, which may include groups, levels, or even individuals. Although the survey data is inconclusive because respondents were from a mix of unionised and non-union companies, data from the ESB and Waterford Crystal tends to suggest that the critical mass also includes union representatives and shop stewards. Certainly, in many change efforts there is a clear sense of having a critical mass of support for change, while in others the lack of support by key clients is seen as a major block to the process.

> It is not so much a question of selling the change, but getting buy-in — many people are cynical; they have been there before — we need to get the cynics involved.

4.2 UNREALISTIC TIMESCALE FOR CHANGE

Post-hoc reviews of major construction projects like the Channel Tunnel and the Sydney Opera House attest to the fact that most of them take twice as long as originally budgeted. Not only are most managers over-optimistic about the timescale for transition — tending to see it as a step-by-step programme or series of projects rather than a messy and time-consuming process — but two intervening variables add to the timescale for change: loss of energy and lack of resources.

LOSS OF ENERGY

As Moss Kanter suggests in *The Change Masters*, "Most projects look like a failure half way through."[2] Concluding that most successful innovations are brought about by those who persist a little longer, she suggests that many projects run out of steam because those involved don't see the benefits in the timescale they expect. Other change efforts seem to hit a wall because the initial stages of implementing new technology, upgrading systems or changing structures are relatively straightforward, while the real challenges are in developing a culture that supports new work practices, teamwork or a different style of managing.

> We can get the structural stuff done in a year and a half. The cultural change will demand a lot more work and at least four years to achieve.

Paradoxically, keeping up the energy for a change process often means overloading people with events, tasks and projects to engage the key clients, while at the same time slowing the process down sufficiently to manage critical process issues like getting people on board, letting go of the past, lowering resistance, and dialoguing through the confusion that often accompanies change. Sustaining the energy during any transition also means building in mechanisms for reviewing the process, celebrating progress, and tackling the "nay sayers".

Examples of Transition Tasks

- Identifying a series of mid-term projects

- Using action plans/Gantt charts to schedule projects and tasks

- Regular progress reviews — cluster groups, conferences, presentations

- Reviewing managers on their supervision of change projects

- Setting up communications channels, newsletters, intranet

- Communicating good news on progress

- Celebrating milestones

- Regular workouts to reduce costs/inefficiencies

- Surveys and audits of attitudes and opinions

- Performance management/career planning, counselling

- Training managers and staff in project-management skills

- Involving many people in task groups, project teams, implementation groups

- Tracking and publicising progress in areas for improvement

- Setting up audit teams to measure progress on implementation

- Fast piloting the change in areas where success is more likely.

One way of sustaining energy during a lengthy transition process is identifying milestones along the way to remind people that progress is being made, while shorter-term targets and deadlines and frequent feedback can also help those involved to recognise that change is an evolving process rather than a time-bounded project. Finally, opportunities for dialogue, including off sites, written briefings, reaffirmation of the vision and frequent staff/management meetings are important ways of maintaining focus and energy over the long haul where new people may be coming on board, leaving or assuming new positions during the process.

The project took over eighteen months to implement. Many of the people involved left the company, which made it difficult to keep focused over such a lengthy period of time.

LACK OF RESOURCES

Bringing about significant change usually requires additional resources being made available in the form of time, staff and money; and lack of resources can often slow the process down to the point where people lose energy or feel that they are unsupported by the top. While creating "slack resources" in the form of additional personnel or consultants is one way in which organisations make space to manage continuous improvement processes, other more bounded changes, with a beginning and an end, often require the creation of additional resources for the duration of the change. In the Arthur D. Little study, of the 350 executives surveyed, over 80 per cent identified themselves as wearing a new hat in relation to the change, as a sponsor, leader or member of a planning team, and 45 per cent also estimated that they spent at least half their work time on change-related activities. Three of the five case examples in this report also recognised in very practical ways the need to make additional resources available for planning and implementing change — in the case of Irish Life and Waterford Crystal, by releasing a significant number of key personnel to work full time on the transition process.

Another way in which organisations commit resources to change is by creating additional structures to ensure that sufficient staff time is scheduled for the process. Regular meetings of a transition team, the use of task groups and project teams, regular management briefings and occasional meetings of a steering committee often form part of the structure for managing change. In the same way that most personal challenges — such as passing exams or getting fit — are achieved by structuring time in the day and week to make them happen, so change processes often get blocked because they lack adequate staff resources or sufficient time scheduled to manage the process.

But apart from time and staff, another critical block to change is the lack of investment in education and retraining. As indicated earlier, investing time and money in education and training materially assists most change efforts. Furthermore, while many organisations invest heavily in technical training to familiarise their staff with new systems and technology, it is often in the softer competencies like coaching, presentation skills, project management and teambuilding that the real investment needs to take place.

> The biggest block to change is lack of commitment at the top to invest in the new skills we require to meet what they say is the strategy for the future.

4.3 LACK OF TRUST

In a similar way to leadership, trust is an important ingredient in most successful change efforts, and one that is easier to define when it is absent than when it is present. Leadership and trust are also related to each other to the extent that when staff-members have confidence in their leadership, they will trust them even when they make tough and painful decisions. In his studies on leadership, Michael Macoby summed up the essential characteristics of good leaders as defined by their followers as "tough but fair".[3] The degree of mistrust that attends many change processes frequently resides in three areas: the emotional baggage of previous failed efforts; a lack of vision for the change and poor internal communications between management and staff.

FAILED ATTEMPTS AT CHANGE

A number of writers refer to the emotional baggage that accompanies many change efforts where mistrust is a major block to transition. As with statements made at job reviews or selection interviews, staff-members are acutely sensitive to promises that were made by management which were not delivered, to mixed messages that confused the real nature of change, and to face-saving retractions from management when staff-members were misled into believing that a painful transition process would lead to a better place.

> When we were floated, we went through a cost-reduction programme. It was tough, basically a 20 per cent cost reduction. When it was done, the chief executive announced that they needed another cost reduction — we felt betrayed.

Building trust and dealing with a legacy of mistrust are critical elements in any bounded change process and also key to developing strong cultures of continuous improvement. Conversely, lack of trust is one of the major covert issues in change, not only residing in the collective subconscious, but often difficult to raise and deal with. It is sometimes suggested that one of the main aims of any change process is to raise and deal with the covert issues — "to make the undiscussable issues discussable". However, while it is usually better to surface and confront under-lying issues rather than have them simmering below the surface, managers are often inclined to push ahead with change in the hope that these issues will diminish over time. Unfortunately, attempting to drive change forward against a hostile workforce often adds to the level of mistrust about management's real intentions and is likely to present itself in more overt forms of resistance and sabotage.

The degree of trust that needs to accompany any change effort usually requires the development of more open relationships between management and staff, between strategic groups, between bosses and staff — and developing those relationships takes time. In the early stages of any process, there is a need to increase contacts and dialogue between those involved in, and affected by, the change, whether through off-site meetings, anonymous griping sessions, diagonally sliced task groups, skip-level meetings, presentations by senior managers and key staff, or other methods that allow staff to share their views and discharge their feelings.

LACK OF VISION OR A PROCESS

Some of the mistrust associated with change is allayed when the facts are made clear or the vision, strategic milestones or steps are laid out before the staff. Not only does it help to spend time at the start of any change process clarifying the need for change and the vision, strategy and implementation process, it also helps that everyone gets the same message at the same time. Proponents of "whole systems change", such as Danemiller–Tyson and Weisbord, support the idea of getting large groups of staff together at the beginning of any change process to hear the same message, debate the change issues, and make their hopes and concerns explicit. Large-scale events are often facilitated by an external consultant, and some organisations build several of them into a process so that people aren't brought together only when there is something critical to announce.

- The necessity for demerging the organisation is clear. Dividing the group in two is the way forward. While one group has clear direction, the second group lacks a story to hang the change around.

- People conspired to make sure it didn't happen — there was a bad process — there was no energy around it.

INADEQUATE INTERNAL COMMUNICATIONS

While senior management may have a clear vision and strategy for the change, unless it is shared at all levels, it often adds to a view that managers are conspiring to change things without consultation or concern for the staff. Moreover, it is easy for managers who are deeply involved in the planning process to forget that it is more important to have buy-in than to come up with the best plan.

As previously discussed, in any transition there is generally a need to overload the organisation with activities to pull people away from their overconcern with operational matters. One strategy for refocusing staff on the future is to increase substantially the amount of information about the change. When SAS went through a major transformation in the 1970s, CEO Jan Carlzon preached simple messages to convince his staff of the need for change. The process was considerably enhanced by a range of illustrated booklets that reinforced those messages.

As part of its continuous change process, Intel gets all the staff together on a bi-annual basis where managers are obliged to give spontaneous answers to questions from the floor, without the opportunity to prepare or massage their responses. Waterford Crystal has bi-annual meetings with its entire staff, 100 at a time, holds 8-weekly team briefings and a weekly meeting of representatives from different parts of the plant. With a smaller number of staff, the Equality Investigations Agency uses weekly staff meetings to reinforce the vision, while at ITG Card Services there are regular monthly change meetings to focus attention on the longer-term issues, and weekly meetings to review progress in the short term.

4.4 LACK OF READINESS FOR CHANGE

In their desire or anxiety to push ahead with the process, senior managers often ignore or minimise the lack of readiness for change.

In his writings on corporate transition, William Bridges[4] suggests that any change process begins with endings that need to be managed before people are psychologically ready to move on to new beginnings, stressing the need for people to let go of the past if they are to move on to a better future. It is tempting to believe that work practices that have been around for years can be rapidly dismantled in favour of a new business model, new technology or systems. However, there is also a requirement for a process to help people to get ready for change and to legitimise their resistance or loss as part of that process.

PROBLEMS WITH LETTING GO

In her seminal work on death and dying, Elizabeth Kubler-Ross identified seven stages that people go through as they come to terms with death, starting with denial and continuing through to acceptance.[5] That model also helps describe one of the major blocks to change — a lack of realisation by management that people need time and help in coming to terms with change, whether to a different business model or to a new technology.

READINESS AT POWERGEN

While there has been a tradition of negotiated change within the ESB, there is now a process at Powergen (the generation division), to radically change work practices and culture. With the phasing out of solid-fuel stations and proposed deregulation by 2005, there is a narrow window of opportunity for Powergen to get ready for a more competitive future.

The emerging process at Powergen recognises the need for a dual approach, accepting that negotiated change is no longer sufficient for the new conditions. The overall process for improving competitiveness and managing transformation — PACT — includes a change-enabling team, CET, and a culture change team, CCT, with a project manager and six internal consultants working with the power stations on identifying and actioning their development plans.

Creating readiness for change is a key issue in Powergen where most managers and staff still cling to a view that the company will always compromise rather than see the lights go out. In this climate, the change team has been learning how to create readiness in non-coercive ways, working to establish a clear vision for the future and getting station managers on board with the need for them to manage the process.

Over the next year, the change team and management group will have to create more urgency for change, rather than wait for deregulation, closures and job losses to reduce their options. So far, various interventions have been undertaken to destabilise managers and to prepare them for the future — such as 360-degree appraisals, individual development plans, career counselling and ISO 1400. Although they have gone some way, there is a huge challenge ahead for Powergen in getting managers and staff to start walking the talk and coming more actively on board with change.

Even when there has been a history of change in an organisation, each transition requires a process to help people let go and move on to the future (losing one parent last year does not mean that you don't grieve the loss of the other this year). While some organisations use ceremony and celebration to help people to accept the need to move on, it is important that managers recognise that it takes time and requires a variety of approaches, such as giving staff opportunities to talk about the past and the future, offering career counselling or transition workshops, and making it legitimate for people to express their anger or frustration without the threat of punishment or being marginalised.

> One of the annoying things about a change process is people changing their minds where you seem to have agreement and then they don't accept. It is a mental process. You are better to back off and give them time — having a major bust up rarely works — you have got to allow people time to take their jumpers off.

Not only does change imply letting go and moving on, it may also require confronting issues such as the current management mind-set or existing practices and norms that may be dysincrinous with the required changes. Moreover, it is easy to presume that everyone is on board with a new system or business model when, in fact, they are acquiescing. While it is tempting to believe that people become institutionalised into existing practices or mind-sets, only after years of being in the same job, the following comment comes from a manager in an organisation that is less than five years old:

> The biggest difficulty we have is getting the mind-set of people to change from the old school to a new focus and new people.

OVERT AND COVERT RESISTANCE

One important piece of learning by many managers in this study was a realisation that people resist change whether it is good or bad. However, while managers are inclined to view resistance as a negative aspect, it also plays a positive role in slowing things down sufficiently to ensure that the champions and advocates of change don't move too quickly and that people who need to be on board have time to get their heads around the process. Furthermore, resistance should remind managers that if they push harder, they will get even more resistance.

Several writers identify a range of strategies for dealing with resistance, one being to force things through and deal with the consequences or to smooth things over in the hope that keeping a lid on the resistance will prevent it from boiling over into reaction. In reality, both strategies often lead to less obvious forms of resistance, such as withdrawal from the process or using busyness and confusion as excuses for not engaging with change.

A third and more productive approach to managing resistance is to confront and resolve the issues that are blocking readiness, by getting them out in the open and dealing with people's fears and concerns even if it is painful. The fight/flight syndrome, or primitive stress response, suggests that when people are anxious, they resist in one of two ways — either by overt resistance or by passive compliance — and both can be substantial blocks to change. Acknowledging the psychological aspects of change, educating managers to recognise and manage resistance, finding ways to reduce the anxiety that accompanies change, and helping people to become more comfortable with instability are better strategies for dealing with resistance than letting it drag the process down until a crisis leaves little option but to employ the very strategies that people feared in the first place.

- Experts were brought in to help on every aspect of our change process except the people.

- A number of people have worked in a culture of stability for many years — it is difficult to change the mind-set that everyone has to change.

One of the more useful diagnostic frameworks in change management is force-field analysis. As a descriptive model, it suggests that, in any transition process, while there are driving forces that are pushing for the change, there is also an equal set of restraining forces that are preventing it from happening. The model suggests that increasing the driving forces and reducing the restraining forces are both ways of facilitating the process in moving forward. (Chapter 4 has described in some detail the main drivers and blocks to change while Chapter 6 moves on to take a look at the benefits and lessons that Irish managers have learned from trying to manage both sets of forces.)

THE BENEFITS AND LESSONS
OF CHANGE

5.1 THE SUCCESS INDICATORS

While the most obvious long-term success indicators of change are improvements in bottom-line results, few organisations initiate a change process simply to improve their short-term profitability. Moreover, although some of the reported external drivers for change suggest that there are significant financial benefits to be gained from new technologies and systems, equally important reasons for change are to keep pace with the new enabling technology, match the competition and retain good staff.

While the Arthur D. Little study, referred to in Chapter 4, indicated that less than 30 per cent of change efforts have any real effect on bottom-line results, this study suggests a more optimistic view in Irish organisations. From examining the driving forces, it is clear that most change is a response to external events, such as an increased demand for products or services, or the availability of new competitive technologies, and profits are a measure of how well organisations respond to the challenges. However, while they are an important measure, bottom-line results are imprecise at best. Other, less well-developed measures — such as improvements in customer retention, longevity and organisational capability — are equally good indicators of success, although more difficult to define and subjective in nature. In reality, faced with a crisis, most organisations can improve their bottom line by reducing headcount, divesting parts of the business and cutting service levels. History tends to record, however, that turnaround strategies may rescue a business from short-term crisis or possible collapse, but will probably have little impact on its long-term survival.

5.2 BENEFITS EXPECTED AND RESULTS ACHIEVED

While the real measures of change are often less tangible and longer term, so too, it appears, are most people's expectations from their change initiatives. Although they were at various stages of a transition process, nearly 75 per cent of the respondents in this survey felt that their company had achieved at least 50 per cent of what it had set out to achieve, and almost 40 per cent indicated that their organisations had achieved above 80 per cent of the results they expected. So, what did they expect and what was achieved? Interestingly, most of the reported benefits were in the less tangible areas like changed attitudes, improved communications and increased levels of customer satisfaction, while more tangible improvements in revenue and profit, reduced costs and better systems were well down the list of perceived benefits.

THE MAIN BENEFITS OF CHANGE (IN RANK ORDER)

1. Changed behaviours
2. Better communications flow
3. Increased customer satisfaction
4. More customer focused
5. Shared information at all levels
6. Speed-up in production, delivery and follow-up
7. Increased revenue or profit
8. Changed relationships — e.g. staff, customer and suppliers
9. New behaviours
10. Better integration
11. Better-educated and informed workforce
12. Better systems

The findings, which suggest that many of the recognised benefits of change are in the less tangible areas, tend to support a view that the real business of change is sustaining a climate of continuous improvement, and periodically re-aligning the organisation with the anticipated needs for the future. However, whether the soft or hard issues are the real agenda for change, the benefits of any change process are difficult to measure. Firstly, in a fast-moving and competitive environment, change isn't so much an option as an imperative — you have to change to survive. Furthermore, while there is a need to make incremental responses to change, a growing number of commentators also subscribe to a view that organisations, large and small, need to embark on more substantial realignments every five to seven years, simply to combat the complacency that has seen so many getting into trouble in recent years — Marks and Spencer, Boots and British Airways, for example.

Pascale is amongst those who comment on the tendency for organisations to blind themselves to the needs of the future by continuing to do a bit more of the same when they are successful, reflecting the view that "success breeds failure". Increasingly, organisations are driven to change not just by immediate threats or incremental opportunities, but as a healthy response to anticipated changes in the future and as a way of avoiding complacency about the present.

> We are driven by uncertainty — that someone will overtake and obliterate the whole payment card system and its technology — the rate of technology change is scary.

As previously suggested, while the desire to improve bottom-line results is seldom the compelling reason for change, it often provides management with a clear objective or a strategic intent to galvanise the effort. Recently, the president of Waterford Crystal committed the company to doubling sales in the next five years, following several previous stretch objectives designed to stimulate a results-driven culture, aimed at restoring optimism after decline and a traumatic turnaround. In summary, while continuous change focuses on making adjustments to the existing systems and processes, most long-term change efforts are aimed at re-aligning the business under such labels as a new business model, a new culture, developing organisational agility, and creating a learning organisation.

5.3 CHANGE CYCLES AND QUICKER RESPONSES

While the environment suggests that change will be an increasing feature for most Irish organisations into the future, it has also to be acknowledged that organisations, like living organisms, tend towards the steady state (homeostasis). As they grow and mature, organisations respond less easily to the changing environment, acquiring as a by-product of their maturity many of the characteristics of bureaucracy that have seen semi-state organisations like Iarnród Éireann and RTÉ having to face externally-driven transformation. While in a more stable environment, mature organisations survive and function adequately, when external conditions shift they are less capable of making the degree of change required of them. In the current environment, these conditions exist for many Irish organisations, and their health can be secured only by establishing change as the norm, through continuous improvement programmes, and by making periodic adjustments to the needs of the future.

The Arthur D. Little study reported eight out of ten managers in the US expecting their companies to be involved in a major change initiative within the next seven years, while the international survey by Carlson Marketing and Gallup (referred to in the Introduction) reported seven out of ten organisations having undergone a major reorganisation within the past five years. In this study, over 75 per cent of the survey respondents expected their companies to be involved in another major change effort within the next two years, and 95 per cent expected that this would occur within five years. Not only does this data reflect a reduction in the time-frame between major re-alignments, but it suggests that, in a developing economy such as Ireland, the time-frame is even shorter for most businesses.

In the same way that the reduction in cycle time from innovation to product development and from development to market has exerted a competitive pressure on business, so too has the need for Irish organisations to reduce their cycle times for managing change. While, in the 1980s, commentators were talking of culture change taking a minimum of five years and incremental change being punctuated by eight- to ten-year frame-breaking changes, the expectation now is that the gap between major re-alignments will shorten. The implication is that organisations will have to learn to manage culture change within a much shorter time-frame and that companies will have to create cultures that are much more responsive to change.

5.4 DEVELOPING LEARNING ORGANISATIONS FOR THE FUTURE

Not only is there an expectation by Irish managers of more change in Irish businesses for the future, but while 33 per cent of the sample in this study felt that their companies were managing change well, almost 60 per cent felt that their companies needed to initiate more change and learn better ways of managing their transitions.

SATISFACTION WITH THE EXTENT OF THE ORGANISATION'S CHANGE EFFORTS	%
Managing change well	37
Need to initiate change and manage it better	57
Doing too much	6

While the qualitative data from the survey reflects a reluctance on the part of many Irish organisations to confront the need for change, there are also indications of a certain degree of complacency about the future. Many organisations continue to hide behind the incrementalist view of change, believing that it will ensure them against having to make major changes down the line. That assumption has been demonstrated by researchers such as Bartunek and Kanter to be incorrect. They clearly show that first order change is generally insufficient to deal with the current speed and level of change, and that organisations will also have to learn to manage periodic frame-breaking changes in order to stay healthy.

> You need to keep telling people, make it public, demystify it and develop a culture of change.

Although the concept of the learning organisation has been around for some time and has been well promoted through the writings of Senge and Pedler, Burgoyne and Boydell,[1] it is only recently that clear links have been established between corporate resilience and organisational learning.

The Shell research project that forms the basis of de Gues's book, *The Living Company*, and the work of Collins and Poras in *Built to Last*,[2] which compared companies that survived beyond fifty years with those that went into decline, suggests some important differences. As the latter study suggests, resilient organisations develop strategies that preserve their core values and ideology, while at the same time introducing mechanisms and structures which allow them to change everything else as the environment demands.

LEARNING TO CHANGE AT WATERFORD CRYSTAL

Having thrived for many years with quality products, a mature market and high wages, Waterford Crystal was rocked to its core by the falling value of the dollar, reduced sales and a downsizing that resulted in a fourteen-week strike. It took a near collapse of the company before the staff voted for fundamental change, which included outsourcing some product, bringing in new managers, a drive on results and a culture change process.

Since 1995, a programme for doubling sales, "Waterford 250", has spearheaded a variety of new structures, systems and personnel. With a clear vision and strategy, a performance-management system that includes personal objectives, frequent reviews and a bonus system based on performance, the company has learned how to survive in a more competitive and uncertain environment.

The transition at Waterford has also recognised the need for a different form of change — "In the past it was obvious — reduce overheads and manpower". The "Waterford Way" has also helped shape the culture to which the company aspires, where the vision and values are shared by all, continuous improvement is the norm, and rewards are equitable and based on performance.

Communications is also a plank in the organisational learning process at Waterford, which includes twice yearly meetings of a joint Irish/US steering committee, bi-annual staff meetings with 100 staff at a time, eight-weekly team briefings and weekly meetings of reps from each area of the plant. It also involves a commitment to a flexible and educated workforce, "who are not happy with what they have".

The creation of a results-driven culture to replace one that was previously dominated by manufacturing has also seen the identification of new management competencies such as teambuilding and values management, an organisational health survey where the results are fed back, department by department, and people having clear roles, accountabilities and performance measures (RAM).

Having learned that standing behind your past successes is no recipe for survival when the environment is changing, Waterford Crystal has managed to forge a new focus on results and flexibility, while preserving its mission to "delight the world with beautiful products".

According to de Gues, as companies increasingly work in environments over which they have less and less control, in order to survive they have to become living and learning communities. Organisational learning includes subscribing to a shared set of values, being open to the outside world, tolerating new ideas and people, and creating a healthy and flexible community. While others have suggested ways in which companies can move in the direction of becoming learning organisations, there is some evidence from the many businesses that have gone into decline that it is not sufficient in today's environment to respond to demand or to improve service and delivery incrementally. Creating a learning organisation means developing appropriate structures, systems, culture and leadership that allow the organisation to raise and deal with fundamental concerns and issues and to continuously enhance its own ability to manage change.

5.5 KEY LESSONS FROM CHANGE

Any hindsight analysis of change is, at best, inexact. As with other destabilising events or shared experiences, those involved are inclined to remember the events rather than what they learned or intuited about the process. Attempts by writers to distil organisational change into a neat set of principles has also tended to present it as an unemotional set of milestones, rather than a disjointed and often messy process, playing down the fact that change is mainly about people who resist anything that makes them uncertain or anxious. However, as managed change begins to figure in the life of most Irish organisations, and as managers develop skills and competencies to deal with transition, a recognition that change is at best a serendipitous process has become more apparent and accepted.

Resisting the temptation to create yet another list of criteria for successful change, this briefing simply comments on the key lessons reported by managers and consultants reflecting on their own experiences with change. In an Irish context, the main lessons for managers are:

1. Learning to deal with change is no longer an option for Irish organisations. Healthy organisations are those that develop the competencies and capabilities to make rapid responses to their changing circumstances.

2. Buy-in and ownership are key to change. Less and less can change be implemented through acquiescence or negotiation. Most of the changes that organisations need to implement for the future require the commitment of staff, and that means involving them in the planning process.

3. Most successful change is led from the top, although it is frequently and significantly managed through the middle.

4. A clear plan or transition process is critical to getting people on board with change, but also as a way of encouraging them to share in the process.

5. It is impossible to bring about substantial change unless time and staffing resources are dedicated to the effort.

6. The longer-term aim of most change efforts is to re-align the culture and strategy with the environment.

1. LEARNING TO MANAGE CHANGE IS NOT AN OPTION

Most change efforts are a response to what is happening in the economic, social, and political environment. While the Irish economy can expect to enjoy continued growth, albeit at a reduced rate, there are various external influences to suggest that it will be a rougher ride for many organisations in the future. With the collapse of the dot.com companies, recession in the US, enlargement of the EU, shortages of skilled labour, changing attitudes on environmental issues, deregulation and national crises like foot and mouth, it is difficult for any Irish organisation to feel certain about the next decade. In an uncertain environment, the best advice is to create organisational architecture that allows for flexibility, responsiveness and agility to whatever external changes occur. As a consequence, the ability to manage change and to create a change culture will be major competitive advantages for Irish organisations in the future.

While developing a culture of change is one of the best ways of ensuring that people at all levels learn to become more comfortable with instability and uncertainty, organisational agility also means changing the management mind-set to one that accepts the need to initiate change before there is a crisis. The old adage, "If it ain't broke, don't fix it", has been well and truly replaced with the maxim, "If it ain't broke, fix it anyway", supporting a view that if your strategy is one of doing more of the same, you are, in effect, sowing the seeds of your own decline. Both Handy (sigmoid curve) and Waterman (weak signals) recognise that the time to initiate change is well before a crisis, which, because of the competitive environment and choices available to customers, may be too late to do anything except employ turnaround strategies to survive.

> In *The Living Company*, Aries de Gues asserts that in a fast-changing world the ability to learn faster than your competitors may be the only sustainable competitive advantage for the future. Many companies fail to learn fast enough: one-third of the companies listed in the Fortune 500 in 1970 had disappeared by 1983.

However, while the main driving forces for change are external, many businesses are only beginning to make use of models for assessing the demands of the environment and identifying the responses they should be making for the future. Although Stakeholder Analysis, Open Systems Planning, the Balanced Scorecard and Benchmarking are frameworks for analysis, there is evidence that many organisations are so focused on immediate responses to customer demand and the competition, that they often miss the big picture which may suggest long-term forces for change, such as shifting demographics, deregulation, technology breakthroughs or re-alignments in the global economy.

2. BUY-IN IS CRITICAL TO SUCCESSFUL CHANGE

Most of the managers in the survey were clear that creating a shared energy for change requires a compelling vision for the future or a crisis sufficient to suggest little option but to change. However, while a vision or a crisis may provide a solid basis for change, it is generally not enough to stop people from wanting to minimise or deny the need. Finding ways to keep key staff almost permanently destabilised through customer surveys, off sites, reviews, audits and benchmarking exercises has become a major factor in creating cultures where organisations remain sensitised to their external environment and ready to move into transition when required.

> In Italy for thirty years under the Borgias they had warfare, terror, murder and bloodshed, but they provided Michelangelo, Leonardo da Vinci and the Renaissance. In Switzerland they had brotherly love, five hundred years of democracy and peace, and what did they produce? The cuckoo clock.
>
> — ORSON WELLES' *THE THIRD MAN*

The twin approaches to creating buy-in and ownership, identified by the survey, include having a clear agenda for change and involving many people in the process. Whether it is a strategic shift or a specific change, critical to gaining buy-in at lower levels is a visible commitment from the top, a clear process for implementation and a shared understanding of the benefits of the changes. It also means managers at all levels knowing what is required of them to meet the changing needs for the future and being actively involved in communicating that commitment even when people are tired of hearing the message.

While it almost goes without saying that communications is critical to achieving buy-in to change, some managers have also learned the importance of quality rather than quantity. Some of the qualitative issues in communicating for change include:

1. *Getting all the facts out into the open.* Bringing the staff together to hear the same messages at the same time and giving them the opportunity to dialogue on the implications is an important

starting point for involvement. Sharing the soft as well as hard data is also critical to convincing groups and individuals — dealing with their views and feelings (hearts and minds) as well as the hard facts. Sometimes it requires a process for raising and dealing with sensitive concerns and external facilitation to make the undiscussable issues more discussable.

2. *Over-communicating.* On the basis that most organisations under-communicate, the key people involved in change have to be overwhelmed with information if they are to be drawn away from their focus on day-to-day issues. Repetition of the same messages also plays an important part in helping people to come to terms with the need for change.

3. *Visible commitment from the top.* Managers must be seen to be actively involved as participants in the process, dramatising the issues, restating the vision, walking the talk and modelling the changes they want to see in others.

4. *Involving many people in the process in many different ways.* During any change or improvement process there is a need to create additional communications structures where people can dialogue, confront issues, challenge their own thinking and actively pursue change through task groups, project teams, off-site meetings, implementation groups, etc.

3. LED FROM THE TOP AND MANAGED BY THE MIDDLES

As suggested earlier, while the prevailing view is that successful change needs leadership from the top, successful implementation often depends on having enough change managers in the middle. Leadership is a somewhat ambiguous term in change because most people confuse "leadership" with "leaders" and much of the literature talks of change leaders at the top and assumes that the same qualities are required by managers lower down the organisation. In reality, even at the top, leadership is often less charismatic and more instrumental than the literature suggests. While most people are familiar with the leadership styles of Richard Branson and Lee Iaccocca, as the authors of *Built to Last* question, "How many people can name the CEO of 3M, probably the most successful and changeable organisation this century?"

Also critical to good leadership at the top is gaining the trust and involvement of middle management. One common feature of many failed change efforts is that senior management plans the change and announces it direct to the workforce, undermining middle management in the process. Not only are middle managers a potential block to change, but they can also be critical to the process, in some cases initiating the change agenda, and in others as a vital element in implementation. Earlier research by this author and others suggests that in many change efforts it is middle managers who are the real initiators and implementors of change, and, as such, those change managers are recognisably different in their attitudes and behaviours from non-change managers. The implication is that, in anticipation of change or as part of the process, those individuals need to be identified and developed as internal change agents or facilitators of change.

4. A CLEAR PLAN OR FRAMEWORK IS IMPORTANT TO THE PROCESS

Apart from having a shared vision or long-term goals, managers in the survey also identified with the need to have a clear process for managing transition. Several managers in the case studies commented on the positive benefits of using external consultants to provide a framework or model, while others commented on the need for a degree of certainty on what is otherwise an uncertain journey into the future.

However, while there are benefits in having a structured approach to managing transition, aided by the usual project-planning techniques, it can have the effect of minimising the importance of the people element in change, particularly where there is mistrust or a legacy of failed efforts from the past. While in some organisations like Intel, where there is a culture of change, the project approach has a history of success, in other organisations, an evolving or action research approach may be more suitable. In practice, most organisations use a combination of both approaches, having an overall plan or framework, while moving the process along with incremental goals, short-term targets and action plans.

5. CHANGE REQUIRES THE CREATION OF SLACK RESOURCES

The principle of "slack resources" suggests one important way for organisations to increase their capacity for change. Any change effort requires additional resources, such as time, staff, money and information, and these are not easy to generate if the organisation is already under pressure from operational demands or the need to reduce staffing levels. Three of the main ways in which companies create additional resources for change include scheduling time, releasing staff and training.

Time: A major reflection from managers in this study was that two of the key ingredients in any change process — planning and communications — can take up a great deal of time, and unless they are scheduled into the process, they simply won't happen. While setting up temporary structures to manage change is important, it is also critical that time be scheduled for off-site reviews, task-group activity and implementation groups.

Managers also learned not to be overambitious with the timescale for change. The inclination on most projects is to take an optimistic view of the time they will take and, when the process comes under pressure, to speed up the implementation at the expense of critical process issues. As such, the unwillingness of staff to commit their time and energies to the effort may have to be confronted head on as a part of the process for pulling them away from their concerns for operational issues, and encouraging them to focus on the change.

Staffing: As reported in the case studies, some organisations create slack resources by assigning people, either full or part time, to the change process. Many Irish companies are also using external resources, such as consultants or facilitators, to provide technical assistance and focus, while others assign staff to change teams, as project leaders, to implementation groups, as internal consultants, or to assignments such as benchmarking or working with outside providers as co-consultants.

The reality that change cannot be managed without time and staff being committed to the effort has been an important lesson for many organisations. It has also encouraged others to recognise that it is difficult to manage change within the existing structures, with existing staffing arrangements and without the investment of a great deal of management time.

Training: A third way in which organisations create additional resources for change is through training. Ireland has seen an unprecedented growth in post-experience education and training during the past decade, a huge investment in multi-skilling and business literacy, and those skills being reflected in selection, induction, training and performance-management systems. Irish companies currently lie in the top 5–7 of European countries for investing in training, second in manufacturing, thanks mainly to the MNCs. However, a recent FÁS report[3] suggests that, if Ireland is to move up the value chain to become a knowledge-based economy, there will have to be a significant increase in the spend on training, simply to keep pace with the increasing investment in other European countries.

While organisations are mainly using training as a vehicle for attracting, training and retraining staff in new technologies and systems, it is also being used as a tool for developing change-related competencies at all levels, such as:

- Job rotation and multi-skilling to create flexibility and prevent employees from settling into inflexible roles or organisational silos

- Training lower-level staff in self-management skills such as business literacy, communications and time management

- Developing teamwork and team-leading skills

- In-house events to share learning — brown-bag sessions, multi-disciplinary projects, benchmarking and presentations

- Developing broader competencies, particularly in the softer skills, such as quality management, customer service and staff relationships

- Using external programmes as development opportunities — e.g. ISO, Excellence through People, and the Quality Mark.

- Non-traditional and lengthier learning events such as outdoors development, competency labs, peer review, and post-graduate qualifications.

In many Irish companies, particularly those in the high-tech sector, staff-members are experiencing a great deal of change in their early career and are being promoted much sooner into management positions. Training in those companies has mainly been aimed at maturing staff to the real business needs and weaning them away from a narrow technical or professional discipline. In some of the more mature companies, including the semi-states and public enterprises, training and education have focused mainly on helping staff to assess their career paths, confront the economic realities of the business and prepare for future transformations where team-work, customer focus, multi-skilling, and value for money will become features of their environment.

6. Change is about Culture as well as Technology, Strategy or Systems

Although many change efforts are ostensibly to introduce new technology, rationalise the product range or gain economies of scale, many of those strategies are linked to changes in the culture. Whether it is changing work practices, improving teamwork, creating shared values, developing a customer focus, or introducing new management styles, one of the important lessons for managers has been the need to destabilise people as a way of moving them forward to new roles, attitudes and ways of working that are more aligned with the tangible needs of the business.

In the current climate, one of the lessons for Irish organisations is the need to find ways to prevent staff at all levels from settling into work practices, roles or structures and to keep them destabilised in whatever ways possible. Although most of the comments in the survey were aimed at managers, many of the lessons learned apply to other levels and to specialist staff. For example:

1. Redefine and renegotiate individual roles at least once a year;

2. Don't let people settle into a routine — e.g. create a range of temporary reassignments, cross-functional projects, and retraining;

3. Insist that managers walk the talk — make their bonuses dependent on managing the values, change projects, and improvements, as at Waterford Crystal and Intel;

4. Develop individual competencies through 360-degree feed-back, retraining, personal development plans (71 per cent of UK companies use performance management to support individual learning and development).

Although most of the reported studies on change management come from the private sector, many recent examples have been in the mature public-sector utilities such as Aer Lingus, Iarnród Éireann, RTÉ, the ESB and Telecom Éireann (Eircom). The prevailing climate in these companies, as they move towards market-driven conditions, dictates that while some things can be negotiated — like staffing levels, compensation for job losses or alterations to working conditions — others cannot. The sorts of changes that many organisations are trying to manage — such as customer focus, safety, on-time delivery, innovation and flexibility — are aspects of culture that cannot be negotiated, and bringing them into the industrial relations arena tends to devalue them.

- They all agree that the biggest stumbling block is the difficulty of changing the culture.

- A large number of the staff have worked for most of their lives in a culture of stability. It is really difficult to change the mind-set that everyone has to change — at the moment we are suffering from severe institutionalisation.

The industrial relations legacy of the 1970s and 1980s has taught many Irish organisations that real culture change can be secured only through mutual trust which is created mainly by involvement, openness, shared information and participation. A history of negotiated change has led some mature Irish organisations to a culture where all change is negotiated and, in the main, has resulted in very little improvement in productivity. The lesson for Irish managers is that change has been taken out of the industrial relations arena and placed firmly in the management domain. As such, some mature organisations have been successful in recent years in shifting change management from the negotiating table and clearly identifying it as a management responsibility.

Individual managers have learned a great deal from their experiences with change in their own areas, and from organisation-wide transitions. They will take these lessons to other jobs and into other companies. At this time, Irish managers and organisations no longer need to go outside the country for examples of effective change management or best practice. In addition, most managers and organisations increasingly recognise that change is a process, part rational and part messy, not aimed solely at managing specific improvements, but targeted also at building capacity for change in line with the prevailing environment and the practices of more resilient and changeable organisations.

CHANGE FOR THE FUTURE

Against a backdrop of rapid and sustained growth in the 1990s, what is the future for organisational change in the next decade? While the ESRI and the Central Bank are currently predicting a continuing growth rate of 2–3 per cent per annum, it is less predictable events such as 11 September, environmental crises like foot and mouth, and political upheavals that will have the greatest effect on our development for the future.

One of the analogies sometimes used to describe the global environment is "white-water rafting", where in past decades organisations could anticipate periods of exhilarating progress, interspersed with occasional rapids and the sometimes becalming effects of the shallows. This view has given way in recent years to what commentators have described as "permanent white water" where constant turbulence is interspersed with unpredictable crises and hidden obstacles. However, while it often seems to previous generations that things were more certain in the past, as one commentator suggests, we have been learning to live with the current environment since the early 1980s.

6.1 FUTURE DRIVERS OF CHANGE

Comparing the present economy with that of a decade ago suggests that the drivers of change in the next decade will be equally significant and different. Moreover, while some external influences are easier to predict — such as the emergence of new breakthrough technologies, enlargement of the EU, the growth of multiculturalism and a more open economy — other influences are less easy to anticipate.

Several commentators believe that the softer issues will become more critical drivers for the future, suggesting that while technology defined the 1990s, so consumerism and a shortage of experienced knowledge workers will have major impact in the next decade. With increasing consumer choice, the globalisation of manufacturing and the commoditisation of many goods and services, a major external driver for the future will be the relationship between the organisation and its customers. In a recent survey by Wharton Business School, the two most critical priorities for the twenty-first century, as judged by an international forum of business leaders, were "providing good customer solutions and a positive experience", and "all the activities of the organisation being directed at adding customer value".[1]

GROWING PAINS AT ITG

Since its establishment in 1989 as a third-party telephone-maintenance company, ITG has grown rapidly and diversified into telecommunications, computer training and supplying "pay per click" facilities as part of the card services sector. Much of that growth has come through acquisition.

ITG has recently restructured its business into separate divisions in the interest of encouraging them to be more strategic and easier to manage. However, while it has simplified the structures, these changes have created issues that the company is only beginning to recognise. One of the major limits to continued growth is the lack of available talent. With competitor companies trawling the same skills pool and a shortage of experienced staff, there is a clear need for the company to grow more rounded talent for the future.

Integration also presents a challenge for the group if it is to gain synergies between the divisions. It has lead to demands for a more strategic focus in the group, which until now has been incremental and opportunistic. Also, for a company that has grown through technology, there are signs that it will have to focus more of its energies on building customer relationships and delivering reliable after-sales service.

While the competition for market share in Ireland and the UK has sustained a momentum in ITG, the appointment of a HR/OD manager is one sign of the future need for better organisational responses. Like many growing companies, ITG has a culture of flexibility and reaction, which, although a strength, has also led to frustrations for staff and customers alike. In a prevailing climate where qualified staff-members have never been in shorter supply and where customer demand is not just for technology but for service and delivery, senior managers are aware that continued growth has to be matched by a shared vision, and supported by good systems, training, an appropriate management style and the retention of good people.*

* Since this case history was completed, the group has divided into two companies, one continuing to deal with existing technologies, and a new company focused on new technologies and applications.

Not only will developing good customer relationships remain an imperative for the next decade (according to research, it costs eighteen times more to create a new customer than to keep an existing one), attracting and retaining good staff will also become a much more demanding driver of change. While the recent book, *After the Celtic Tiger*,[2] suggests that the economic growth of the 1990s, was facilitated mainly by employment growth, in a fully employed economy, productivity growth will become a much more critical issue for the future.

> The key to economic success in the long run is the more efficient use of available resources, especially labour, rather than the employment of additional resources at the same level of efficiency....
>
> The forces that drive productivity growth are widely recognised. The ideal combination is a well-educated and adaptable labour force working with new technologies and up-to-date physical capital (such as machinery and buildings).
>
> — *After the Celtic Tiger*

The suggestion that Irish organisations will be driven to make better use of scarce labour resources is also confirmed by data from the case-interviews, which identified the need to reduce costs and improve results as overriding concerns for many organisations. Findings reported by Collins in *Good to Great*,[3] also support the view that "Getting the right people on the bus, the wrong people off the bus, and the right people in the right seats" is critical to sustaining long-term productivity growth and competitive advantage.

Not only will the drive for productivity and competitiveness determine the shape of Irish organisations in the next decade, but organisations will also have to accommodate changing attitudes to work and home life. A recently published *Sunday Times* supplement, "100 Best Companies to Work For"[4] reports that organisations that are most highly rated by their staff do not rely on financial incentives to attract and retain good people, but rather treat their staff with respect through openness, trust, loyalty and hands-off management. The report suggests that not only are participation and openness good for holding on to good staff, but they relate directly to productivity and growth (in the past five years, the 100 best companies to work for have grown by an average of 25.45 per cent, year on year, compared with 6.3 per cent for the FTSE all share index).

Changing social attitudes in Ireland will also have a major effect as drivers of change in the next decade. Obvious signs of increased spending power, such as second-home ownership, new-car registrations, and multiple overseas holidays, reflect the current choices being made by many Irish people. While employment and job security were high on the agenda for families in the 1980s and 1990s, those issues have given way to more qualitative concerns — affordable housing, traffic congestion, environmental control and quality of work life. Furthermore, although some Irish organisations have responded to those needs by introducing flexi-time, part-time work, and remote working, the longer hours and commuting times experienced by many workers have led to a reappraisal by individuals and society alike. Indications are that the price people were willing to pay for full employment in the 1990s is one that they will be less prepared to accept in the next decade.

6.2 FUTURE RESPONSES

One interesting thesis in the book, *Good to Great*, is that it takes time to build momentum in an organisation or an economy. Using the example of the fly wheel, which takes a great deal of time to get going before it develops its own energy, the suggestion is that the essentials which led to the Celtic Tiger of the 1990s were put in place mainly during the 1970s and early 1980s. Following the line of this thesis, the indications are that it will require new competencies for the future if organisations are to sustain the momentum of the past decade.

While the challenges to retain customers, reduce costs and increase employee productivity will remain significant for the future, building on the successes of the past decade will also require a new set of organisational design assumptions.

> Traditionally the purpose of organisational structures was to institutionalise stability; in the organisations of the future the goal of design will be to institutionalise change.
>
> — *Driving Change*

Some years ago, Rosabeth Moss Kanter suggested that successful organisations of the future would be: Faster, more Focused, Flatter, Flexible and Friendly (see Chapter 4, page 45). While many Irish organisations have been busy during this decade keeping pace with increased demand for their products, introducing new technologies and attracting staff, in the next decade there will be a major shift of emphasis in the directions she indicates.

FASTER

While the development cycles of most products and services have reduced considerably in this decade, prompting a drive for constant innovation and redesign, organisations also have to make rapid responses to external events, such as environmental controls, break-through technologies and new entrants to the market. As recently witnessed in industries as diverse as insurance, airlines and cement, new entrants can capture a significant slice of the market with-out having to go through the traditional stages of growth and development.

Not only will response time to innovation, development and delivery become an increasing advantage for the future, aided by fast pilots, the Internet, CAD and instant communications, but organisations will also have to learn to make faster re-alignments to the environment. Rather than anticipating major change every six to ten years, Irish organisations will have to learn to cope with that level of transition every two to three years, while maintaining con-tinuous improvement in innovation, lead times and response to customer needs. In addition, while "faster" means learning to antici-pate and manage change more quickly, it also means developing the organisational architecture (structures, systems, culture and work practices) to accommodate that level of flexibility and responsiveness.

FOCUSED

While a great deal of the growth in Irish organisations over the past decade has been the result of new technologies, increased demand and mergers, Irish organisations will increasingly have to focus on creating sustainable value through developing their core compe-tencies, such as time to market, delivery, quality and service.

Central to the process of becoming more strategic and resilient for the future will be the identification of areas of competitive advantage that appeal to customers and staff and differentiate the organisation from the competition. While those competencies are likely to be in the softer areas, the critical challenge for the future will be leveraging them through developing and embedding a core ideology, identifying and developing focused areas of activity, developing values-driven leadership at all levels, designing appropriate rewards systems, and involving all the stakeholders in continuous improvement and change.

FLATTER

Although many Irish companies have already gone through the exercise of reducing costs by pruning bureaucracy and excess staff, the intended benefits have yet to be realised by most. Keeping close to the customer and empowering lower levels of staff to manage the customer relationship mean that organisations must promote values that support risk-taking, develop recruitment and training policies which reflect their espoused values and style, and find ways to reward the attitudes and behaviours they want to encourage.

Reducing levels of hierarchy and pushing more responsibility to the customer interface will also put greater pressure on organisations to integrate the effort across the boundaries in the form of matrix structures, multi-skilling, cross-functional teamwork, the elimination of organisational silos and a greater focus on shared values.

FLEXIBLE

Although the development of the Irish economy has not been held back significantly by the burden of large mature industries, there are clear signs in the public and semi-state sector of the need for renewal and revitalisation. One of the major blocks to industrial growth in the future will be the lack of good and efficient infrastructure such as public transport, telecommunications, roads, and the increasing costs of energy.

In both the private and public arenas, the task of making goods and services accessible at competitive prices to a more discerning and demanding customer base will put increased pressure on developing "go-to-market" flexibility through one-stop shops, the Internet and e-commerce, tailor-made packages, relationship marketing and service at all levels. Within organisations, developing the flexibility to make rapid responses to changes in technology and the market will also lead to broader and more flexible roles at all levels and to an increasing emphasis on cost, quality and service.

FRIENDLIER

One of Jack Welch's more pithy comments — that, in traditional hierarchy, "people have their noses to the CEO and their asses towards the customer"[5] — also suggests need for radical change in the next decade. As John Scully, former CEO of Apple, currently running a network of informal organisations, suggests, "It isn't how you design the organisation that matters, it is being able to reach your customers to their satisfaction, and that is mainly an issue of culture and style."[6]

ORGANISATIONS OF THE FUTURE

FLATTER
— Fewer levels, more responsibility
— Closer to the customer
— Better horizontal integration/between the boundaries
— Cross-functional teamwork

FLEXIBLE
— Strategic alliances/partnerships
— Greater use of enabling technology/IT
— Continuous feedback and adjustment/customers/staff
— Broad roles, multi-skilling and more involvement

FASTER
— Time as a major competitive advantage
— Increase in experimentation/fast pilots
— Creating organisational agility/ability to change fast
— Instant communications/direct/internet/CAD

FOCUSED
— Less management, more leadership/self-direction/specific rewards
— Distinctive advantages in soft areas, service, quality
— Preserve core ideology/flexible to change all else
— Outsourcing of non-core activities

FRIENDLIER
— Relationship building/customers and suppliers
— Listening/quicker responses to staff and customers
— Initiatives on staff retention/growth and development
— Style/fun/great place to work

While the customer-service message has been taken on board by many Irish companies and is part of their competitive advantage, it must become more integrated into the processes for sustaining customer relationships (CRM), through acting on customer feedback, informal networking, staff retention policies, creating a distinctive style and better management of the supply chain. Achieving the level of performance that customers are increasingly coming to expect also implies developing more openness, trust and the greater involvement of staff in the process.

6.3 CHANGE MANAGEMENT (CM) FOR THE FUTURE

Any predictions of where change management is going for the future are necessarily based on changes in the environment, the current trends in organisation design, and the literature on CM. While it is tempting to suggest a number of possible scenarios, the certainties for CM in the next decade will be in four areas:

1.   Change management will increasingly focus on changing mind-sets, culture and the softer competencies, as well as technology, systems and strategies;

2.   Direction will continue to be set at the top, while CM strategies will increasingly involve people from below, including staff, customers and suppliers;

3.   Change management will shift its focus to building organisational architecture for competitive advantage, rather than on dealing with external or internal crises, or implementing programmed approaches to change;

4.   There will be more concern in organisations for developing long-term strategies for institutionalising change. As such, there will be more emphasis on balancing the economic realities of change with issues that also need to be dealt with if change is to be successful.

1. INCREASING FOCUS ON CHANGING CULTURE AS WELL AS TECHNOLOGY

In the past decade, Irish organisations have mainly been driven to change by unprecedented levels of demand and increased competitiveness. In response, many have introduced new communications and information technology, developed better systems, and radically changed their marketing and operational strategies. Supporting those changes have been programmes and processes including ISO, TQM, BPR, CRM and other less proprietary approaches to improving service, quality and innovation. The recognition that many of these programmes have not fulfilled their promise has prompted many Irish organisations to re-examine and modify their approaches to CM.

Increasingly, organisations and managers are aware that in order to achieve the benefits of change, it is important that they deal with the softer and less visible aspects of change as well as the harder elements. Attempting to drive change down through the organisation without confronting issues such as existing work practices and norms, denial of the need for change or of staff resentment is not only likely to attract resistance but is at odds with many of the things that organisations need to manage to get real change.

In the current climate, where the advantages of participation, hands-off management styles and improved communication have been well accepted by many organisations, there is a realisation that sustaining those advantages means dealing with change in more enlightened and inclusive ways for the future.

2. DIRECTION FROM THE TOP AND INVOLVEMENT FROM BELOW

Several sources in this briefing — including current research, the survey and interview data — confirm a view that successful CM has to be led from the top and requires buy-in and engagement with all levels below.

While it is clear that change is sometimes initiated and driven from the middle or by specialist departments, it is evident that key to most successful change efforts is leadership from senior management to support and push the process forward. As one change consultant reflected, "I didn't realise how much support we were getting from the top until the MD resigned — within a month I was gone and in a couple of months the process was dead."

However, while change needs to be driven and supported from the top, CM will also have to find better ways to engage with staff at all levels. Because so much of the real change that organisations are trying to bring about requires buy-in from the staff, their early involvement in the planning process is the best way of achieving that commitment. Also, as organisations are increasingly espousing empowerment and pushing responsibility and risk-taking down to lower levels, it would be sending mixed messages if the staff were not involved in the change. In addition, as the pace of change quickens, organisations will be increasingly vulnerable to competitors making inroads into their business if staff-members are blocking changes they need to make in order to match that competition.

3. Focus on Building the Architecture for Change

While organisations traditionally required an impending crisis or new leader with a vision to stimulate change, the new focus will be on anticipating the future and making contingencies for possible scenarios. To remain healthy and competitive in a turbulent and rapidly changing environment, organisations will have to develop technologies, structures, systems and activities that help them to identify potential issues and opportunities well before they become a reality and to act on them speedily.

While it is evident that many organisations have already gone some way along the path of creating a capability for change, some of the features that help to develop changeability include having a shared vision for the future, continually challenging existing mind-sets on ways of doing business, improving teamwork, better boundary management, elimination of organisational silos, involvement at all levels in planning, continuous improvement processes, measurement of soft and hard issues, greater use of IT in strategy development and communications, increased business literacy, environmental scanning, and developing structures and systems for listening to both customers and staff.

4. Better Fit between CM Processes

For the future, it is likely that there will be increasing synergy between top-down results-driven change and bottom-up change aimed at developing corporate culture, human capacities and new behaviours and attitudes. On the one hand, top-down approaches to change can achieve quick results, but this is often at the expense of future capability. On the other hand, change strategies aimed at developing competencies and attitudes take time and can prevent the organisation and managers from making the tough decisions that they may need to make for the future.

Both Kilman[7] and, more recently, Beer and Nohria[8] suggest that organisations need to get beyond the quick fix and to start using approaches that get results but also build capacity for change. In doing so, organisations will have to find ways to accommodate both strands of CM — top-down and bottom-up — possibly by sequencing them in the change process in such a way that time and attention are given to the soft as well as the hard issues. Alternatively, companies could put more effort into building up the softer side of the organisation in terms of developing mind-sets, attitudes, flexibility and human systems that will more easily accommodate the harder, more rational side of change.

While some Irish organisations have embraced new models and practices in relation to CM, developing their capacity from within, others will continue with programmed approaches to change, while others rely on turnaround strategies that include replacing managers, reducing staff levels and cutting costs. It is clear from a combination of sources that while some Irish organisations are learning to develop new tools and strategies to deal with the evolving conditions for change, others will continue to operate on the maxim, "If the only tool you have is a hammer, you treat everything as if it were a nail." However, while organisations may have responded differently to the new conditions, it is reassuring that many companies during the past decade have moved away from simplistic and top-down approaches in favour of more managed and inclusive strategies for change.

6.4 CHANGE MANAGERS OF THE FUTURE

Although it is early days to assess the extent to which Irish businesses have become learning or changeable organisations, there is a sense that many are managing their agenda for change in more mature ways than in previous decades. This is a result, in large part, of companies operating in more open and competitive environments, benchmarking their activities against industry leaders, their managers gaining more international experience, investment in management education and development, and companies and managers learning how to deal with change through the school of hard knocks.

Attending the seed shift in the way that companies are dealing with change have been developments in the managers' role. While it is clear that, in times of change, organisations need more leaders and leadership at all levels, as Nadler and Tushman suggest, the future requirement will be for "polydextrous leadership".[9] Not only will managers be expected to maintain superior performance and to initiate changes in targeted areas of the business, but as organisations become flatter and closer to their suppliers and customers, they will have to learn to manage highly differentiated and sometimes competitive parts of the business.

Furthermore, while part of the managers' emerging strategic function is to identify opportunities for growth, to encourage innovation and manage integration, it will also increasingly be about managing change in the softer areas, such as work practices, management style, developing teamwork and embedding values. In companies like Intel, Waterford Crystal and GE, managers are currently rated and rewarded on their management of the values, and at GE that includes being assessed on their ability to communicate the vision, an openness to change, and their success in developing teamwork.

In addition, and related to leadership, is the fact that many Irish organisations have moved along a continuum of managing change by decree and negotiation to change by consultation, involvement and consensus. If a major competitive advantage for the future is the ability of organisations to make rapid responses to changes in the environment, it presupposes that the role of managers will be to utilise their staff better as the key resource that businesses often espouse.

While the human systems concepts advocated in the 1960s — such as autonomous work groups, socio-technical work design, participation, job enrichment and industrial democracy — never realised their promise, a new relationship between workers and managements has begun to emerge in this decade. It has seen practical moves towards participation and involvement that are driven not by humanistic values, but by a real need for customer-friendly design, dedicated knowledge workers, better people management, and by the shortage of skilled staff.

6.5 Conclusion

How well Irish organisations are dealing with change is not easy to establish because, when they are doing well, there is a degree of complacency about change. Also, when change is handled well, it is not so newsworthy, while if it is handled badly, it often leads to turnaround strategies that include reducing staff or divesting parts of the business, and they are much more likely to grab the headlines. However, while the resolution of industrial conflicts and last-minute turnarounds attract a better press than healthy change, the question remains as to how these organisations get into the crises they so brilliantly surmount.

The accumulated data for this briefing, including the case examples, the survey results and the current literature on change, suggest that the past decade has been a huge learning experience for many Irish organisations and managers. While the seeds of the Celtic Tiger were sown in the 1970s and 1980s, it has been the sustained growth in this decade that has allowed, and in some cases forced, organisations to confront the way in which they manage change. With that in mind, the next decade is likely to present even more of a challenge for Irish organisations to maintain the benefits that they have gained, but also to institutionalise new structures, systems, styles and strategies to deal with the turbulent and uncertain times ahead.

REFERENCES

Introduction

1. Carlson Marketing Group and Gallup Organisation Survey, quoted in *Training and Development*, January 2000.
2. Pascale, R., Millemann, M., and Gioja. L. (1997), "Changing the Way We Change", *Harvard Business Review*, November–December.
3. Hunt, J. (2000), "The Change-Able Organisation", *Journal of the Strategic Planning Society*, September.
4. Herman, S. (1994), "A Force of Ones", San Francisco: Jossey Bass.
5. Clegg, C. at al. (1996), "The Performance of Information Technology and the Role of the Human and Organisational Factors", UK: *Report to the Economic and Social Research Council*.

Chapter 1

1. Amos, A.G., and Pascale, R.T. (1981), *The Art of Japanese Management*, New York: Simon and Schuster.
2. Peters, T.J., and Waterman, R.H. (1982), *In Search of Excellence*, New York: Harper and Row.
3. Senge, P. (1990), *The Fifth Discipline*, New York: Doubleday.
4. de Gues, A. (1997), *The Living Company*, London: Nicholas Brealey.
5. O'Dowd, J. (1998), *Employee Partnership in Ireland: A Guide for Managers*, Dublin: Oak Tree Press.

Chapter 2

1. Lewin, K. (1951), *Field Thoery in Social Science*, New York: Harper Brothers.

Chapter 3

1. Mirvis, P. and Berg, D.M. (1977), *Failures in Organisation Development and Change: Cases and Essays for Learning*, New York: Wiley.

2. Kotter, J.P. (1995), "Leading Change: Why Transformation Efforts Fail", *Harvard Business Review*, March–April.

3. Beer, M. (1990), *The Critical Path to Organisational Renewal*, Boston: Harvard Business Press.

4. Kotter, J.P. (1995), "Leading Change: Why Transformation Efforts Fail", *Harvard Business Review*, March–April.

5. Frohman, A.L. and Johnson, L.W. (1993), *The Middle Management Challenge: Moving from Crisis to Empowerment*, New York: McGraw-Hill Inc.

6. Weisbord, M. (1987), *Productive Workplaces: Organising and Managing for Dignity, Meaning and Community*, San Francisco: Jossey Bass.

7. Welch, J. with Byrne, J.A. (2001), *Jack: What I've Learned Leading a Great Company and Great People*, UK: Headline Book Publishing.

8. Pascale, R.T. (1990), *Managing on the Edge – How the Smartest Companies Use Conflict to Stay Ahead*, New York: Simon and Schuster.

9. Nordstrom, K. and Riddertrale, J. (2000), *Funky Business: Talent Makes Capital Dance*, England: Brookhouse Publishing.

10. Collins, J.C. and Poras, J.I. (1996), *Built to Last: Successful Habits of Visionary Companies*, London: Random House.

Chapter 4

1. Little, A.D. (1994), Management Study, "Managing Organisational Change: How Leading Organisations are Meeting the Challenge".

2. Kanter, R.M. (1983), *The Change Masters*, New York: Simon and Schuster.

3. Macoby, M. (1976), *The Gamesman: New Corporate Leaders*, New York: Simon and Schuster.

4. Bridges, W. (1988), *Surviving Corporate Transitions*, New York: Doubleday.

5. Kubler-Ross, E. (1969), *On Death and Dying*, New York: Macmillan Publishing Company.

Chapter 5

1. Pedler, M., Burgoyne, J. and Boydell, T. (1997), *The Learning Company*, London: The McGraw Hill Companies.

2. Collins, J.C. and Poras, J.I. (1996), *Built to Last: Successful Habits of Visionary Companies*, London: Random House.

3. Fox, R. (2002), *Training in Companies – How Does Ireland Score?*, Dublin: FÁS – Training and Employment Authority.

Chapter 6

1. Wind, J. (1999), *Driving Change: How the Best Companies are Preparing for the 21st Century*, London: Kogan Page.

2. Clinch, P., Convery, F. and Walsh, B. (2002), *After the Celtic Tiger*, Dublin: The O'Brien Press.

3. Collins, J.C. (2001), *Good to Great*, London: Random House.

4. *Sunday Times Supplement* (2002), "100 Best Companies to Work For", *The Sunday Times*, March.

5. Welch, J. with Byrne, J.A. (2001), *Jack: What I've Learned Leading a Great Company and Great People*, UK: Headline Book Publishing.

6. Scully, J., verbal comment made at an IMI Conference.

7. Kilman, R.H. (1984), *Beyond the Quick Fix: Managing Five Tracks to Organisational Success*, London: Jossey Bass.

8. Beer, M. and Nohria, N. (2000), "Cracking the Code of Change", *Harvard Business Review*, May–June.

9. Nadler, D.A. and Tushman, M.L. (1999), "The Organisation of the Future: Strategic Imperatives and Core Competencies for the 21st Century", *Organisational Dynamics*, Vol. 28, Issue 1.

APPENDIX

How Organisations Deal with Change

Many thanks for agreeing to complete this questionnaire. Your answers will be confidential. The introductory details are for administrative purposes only.

Please answer the questionnaire as it applies to a current change process in your organisation. If you find that difficult, please complete it in relation to your experiences with change in the company in the past.

Name:
Company: Industry:
No. of employees in company:
Your position (tick one):
Senior manager
Middle manager
Supervisor
Specialist or administration staff

1. **What is the most recent or current change process in your organisation? (limit to 3)**

   ❑ New or upgraded technology
   ❑ Strategic shift, e.g. markets, new alliance
   ❑ New structure or restructuring
   ❑ New systems, e.g. information, MRP, performance management
   ❑ Change in delivery or supply
   ❑ Merger
   ❑ Change in work practices, e.g. teamworking, job redesign
   ❑ New initiative –TQM, ISO, Quality Mark, Excellence through people (indicate which one)

   • Please elaborate overleaf

2. What were/are the main external drivers for the change? (limit to 3)

☐ Technology
☐ Legislation
☐ Take over/merger
☐ Competition
☐ Organisational or industry decline
☐ Market decline
☐ Falling revenues
☐ New leader with a vision
☐ High cost base
☐ Shareholder dissatisfaction
☐ Customer dissatisfaction
☐ Increased demand for product or service
☐ Others (please specify)

3. What stage of the change process are you at?

☐ Getting ready
☐ Halfway through
☐ Finished the transition
☐ Bedding down the changes

4. Who or what were/are the main internal driving forces for the change? (limit to 3)

☐ A particular person/leader/champion
☐ Top management group
☐ Middle management group
☐ Group of managers
☐ Specialist staff, e.g. Human Resources or OD
☐ Other staff
☐ Others (please specify)

5. Did you use external consultants?

❑ Yes/No

For what?
❑ To do a diagnosis/survey
❑ Convince staff of the need for change
❑ Facilitate the process
❑ For technical or financial help
❑ To introduce expert systems
❑ Other reasons (please specify)

6. How has the company/organisation educated and trained managers in change management?

❑ External training
❑ Informal
❑ Consultants
❑ Existing background of change
❑ Others (please specify)

7. From your experience with this change, which factors are critical to implementing change? (rank order top 3)

❑ Leadership at the top
❑ Middle management buy in to the change
❑ A clear vision for the future
❑ Detailed planning of the process
❑ Communications at all levels
❑ Making time to manage the process
❑ Keeping up energy for the process
❑ A critical mass of support for the change
❑ Lack of resistance to the change
❑ Taking it at the right pace
❑ Having key people on board, e.g. middle managers/strategic group
❑ Rewarding people for changing behaviours/practices/attitudes
❑ Celebrating successes along the way
❑ Others (please specify)

8. What specific Tools or Approaches helped the change process? (3 main ones)

- ❑ Training in change management
- ❑ Training in new approaches/skills etc
- ❑ Use of an external consultant
- ❑ Changing the rewards system
- ❑ Having a Transition team
- ❑ Use of task groups/project teams
- ❑ Going for an award
- ❑ Off sites
- ❑ Questionnaires and surveys
- ❑ Measurable targets
- ❑ Others (please specify)

9. What were/are the main blocks in the process? (tick 3)

- ❑ Lack of ownership/buy in
- ❑ Lack of an agreed process
- ❑ Lack of middle level support
- ❑ Length of time it takes/is taking
- ❑ Lack of commitment at the top
- ❑ Lack of readiness for change
- ❑ Lack of enough people supporting the change
- ❑ Lack of a clear crisis or vision
- ❑ Lack of trust
- ❑ Lack of energy for the process
- ❑ Resistance

- ● Explain the main blockage

10. What have been the main benefits of the change in your company over the past year?

- ❑ Changed attitudes
- ❑ New behaviours
- ❑ Changed relationships, e.g. staff, managers, customers, suppliers
- ❑ Customer satisfaction
- ❑ Better integration
- ❑ Better educated and informed workforce
- ❑ Changed climate
- ❑ Speed up in production, delivery and follow up
- ❑ Increased revenue or profit
- ❑ Better communications flow
- ❑ Shared information at all levels
- ❑ Shared vision and values
- ❑ Better systems
- ❑ More customer focused
- ❑ Reduction in costs/increased revenues

11. To what extent have the change efforts produced the results you expected?

- ❑ 100%
- ❑ 80%
- ❑ 50%
- ❑ 30%
- ❑ 10%
- ❑ Not at all

12. What tips would you offer other managers getting into a change process?

13. Are you happy with the extent of your companies change efforts?

- ❑ Managing change well
- ❑ Need to do more to initiate and manage change
- ❑ Doing too much

14. Do you expect to be involved in another major change process in the next:

❑ 1–2 years
❑ 3–5 years
❑ 5–7 years
❑ 7–10 years
❑ Never

Many thanks for agreeing to complete the questionnaire and for your time.

Tom McConalogue

DON*T MESS with a ...ncess!

Rachel Valentine ♛ Rebecca Bagley

OGRE FEST
ROCK FESTIVAL
SAT-SUN
THE SWAMP

CHIP SHOP

For Becky Bagnell, with so many
thanks – R.V.

For my brand new family and the
adventure we've just begun - R.B.

PUFFIN BOOKS

UK | USA | Canada | Ireland | Australia
India | New Zealand | South Africa

Puffin Books is part of the Penguin
Random House group of companies
whose addresses can be found at
global.penguinrandomhouse.com.

www.penguin.co.uk
www.puffin.co.uk
www.ladybird.co.uk

Penguin
Random House
UK

First published 2019
001

Text copyright © Rachel Valentine, 2019
Illustrations copyright © Rebecca Bagley, 2019
The moral right of the author and illustrator
has been asserted

Printed in China

A CIP catalogue record for this book is
available from the British Library

ISBN: 978–0–241–32262–8

All correspondence to: Puffin Books,
Penguin Random House Children's,
80 Strand, London WC2R 0RL

MIX
Paper from
responsible sources
FSC® C018179